Giuseppe Vespignani SDB

A Year at The School of
Don Bosco
1876–1877

Translated by the FMA English-Language Translation Group (ETG)

Don Bosco
Publications

Don Bosco Publications

Thornleigh House, Sharples Park, Bolton BL1 6PQ
United Kingdom

ISBN 978-1-909080-82-9
©Don Bosco Publications, 2022

Un Anno alla Scuola del Beato Don Bosco (1876–1877) Torino: Società Editrice Internazionale, 1930.

Front cover image @SDB.org

Printed in malta by Melita Press

FSC
www.fsc.org
MIX
Paper from
responsible sources
FSC® C004116

Foreword

I have the great privilege of presenting this collection of vibrant Memoirs to the public. They are dedicated to the Salesians, their friends and to hagiographers. For the Salesians, it is enough to remember that it is their beloved scholastic councillor who is speaking. The friends of the Salesians and of their work will undoubtedly be pleased with this wealth of intimate information about Don Bosco, Fr Rua and the early days of the Oratory. As for hagiographers, it will be useful to have a rich documentation of sound historical value that has an important bearing on the subject of their research. Here, we live in an atmosphere saturated with spirituality, and since the witness is absolutely trustworthy, his evidence has been collected in these pages and reproduced with the utmost fidelity. The very abundance of detail, which could have been even greater if so desired, results from the intention of safeguarding historical accuracy.

It is our conviction that the study of Don Bosco and his work has scarcely begun. While it seems that much has already been done, a great deal still remains to do, so that the nature and actions of this star of primary grandeur in the firmament of the Church may be fully revealed. This task will fall to future generations. In the meantime, it is up to us today to preserve and transmit all possible material to these future students, applying the evangelical admonition "gather up the fragments, that they may not be lost" while eyewitnesses still survive.

Eugenio Ceria SDB
Turin, November 15, 1929

Contents

Introduction

The English-language Translation Group (ETG) is an international group of FMA representing various parts of the world. Mother Antonia Colombo, leader of the Institute and her council commissioned the group in 1998. The principal aim of this body is to translate, from Italian, significant primary and secondary source material relevant to the spirituality of the FMA.

During General Chapter XXII in the presence of Mother Yvonne Reungoat, Mother Antonia Colombo and some members of the General Council and the provincials of the English-speaking provinces, the ETG group was re-established.

The ETG decided to prepare a modern translation of Fr Vespignani's *Un Anno alla Scuola del Beato Don Bosco* because of its great value as a first-hand account of life at Valdocco during the lifetime of Don Bosco. It gives a real flavour of his life and that of the early Salesians as well as of the early years on the missions in Argentina. In these years, the Salesian family is becoming ever more conscious of the need for an in-depth understanding of the Preventive System in order to live it and share it. This book is a precious source of that system in its purest form. It also shows Don Bosco's deep interest in each individual Salesian and his care for their formation.

Style and Mechanics of the English Translation

Throughout the text, the ETG has tried to utilise words and terms that are acceptable wherever English is spoken. The group sought agreement on usage and chose that which was most understandable, if not always the most acceptable, for a given country or region.

British English spelling is used throughout the text. The US date sequence is used i.e., month/day/year. In keeping with modern usage, capital letters have been reduced to a minimum. Where necessary, the group chose to transform long sentences into shorter ones. Where possible, terms such as *saving souls, superior* have been replaced by words that are more commonly acceptable today, according to the context (e.g., person, or young people, Salesian or General Councillors). When the word *oratory* is used to signify Don Bosco's first home and works for his boys in Valdocco the editors have used a capital letter. Lower case is used when it refers to the oratory as a ministry. The term *Don* in Italian is a title applied to priests. The editors have used *Don* for St John Bosco (Don Bosco, as he is universally known) and have translated it as *Father* when naming all other priests. Throughout the text, as far as possible, proper names of people are left in their original language. The names of major cities are translated into English; all other place names are left in the original.

This book was written in 1929, the year of the beatification of Don Bosco. For this reason, the author constantly refers to our Founder as *Blessed.* We have chosen to leave this title as it expresses something of the atmosphere in which the book was written.

The ETG does not share the sentiments expressed in certain parts of this text, which was written in a period when ecumenical sensitivity was not as widespread as today. However, to change it would have meant to alter the thought of the author.

Inclusive language and terminology that respects the dignity of all people have been used where possible. At times, in order to respect the thought of the author, some quotes using terminology that would not be commonly used today (e.g., souls, superiors, natives) have not been changed.

The FMA English-language Translation Group
Sr Patricia Devine
Sr Philomena B. D'Souza
Sr Rachel Flor
Sr Edna Mary Macdonald
Sr Maire O'Byrne
Sr Louise Passero

Chapter 1

By the Light of the Lamp

I was a newly ordained priest when I went to Don Bosco to become a Salesian. The ways by which I was led to this goal were providential. I would never have had the strength to make such a decision on my own in view of my shyness, my poor health and the obstacles on the part of my family. All increased the uncertainty of the issue. Only an invisible hand could have led and sustained me thus far to this place where I met a saintly Father, a new family and, above all, a great and beautiful mission. This is the vocation that God inspires in us, his poor creatures; this is the assistance that the Help of Christians gives to those who rely on her maternal care and who confidently go to her for enlightenment, strength and generosity in reaching the goal appointed by Divine Providence for each one of us.

I arrived in Turin at 10pm on November 7, 1876. The carriage left me outside the Church of Mary Help of Christians, but the doors seemed to be locked. I was wondering how to get in when I saw a light in the windows of what was then the Oratory bookstore. I knocked on the first window and asked to be let in, announcing myself as a priest who had come from Alassio looking for Don Bosco. In a few moments, Fr Celestino Durando appeared and, hearing where I came from and why, told me that Don Bosco had just finished hearing the boys' confessions since there was to be a solemn function in the Church for departing missionaries on the next day. He added that he had been having supper with Don Bosco and immediately took me to him.

Upon entering the refectory, I asked him to point out Don Bosco since there were many priests gathered around the table, speaking familiarly among themselves. He took me to the head of the table where I kissed Don Bosco's hand and presented a letter of introduction to the saint. It had been written by Fr Francis Cerruti, Rector of the Salesian school at Alassio. In the letter, he mentioned that I had just accompanied my brothers there. I then reminded him of a letter I had written the previous year asking for accommodation for my younger brothers and said that I was now asking for a place for myself. He remembered everything and had me sit at his right. While my soup was being served, Don Bosco handed Fr Cerruti's letter to Fr Rua, who was beside me at the table. When he read the letter, Fr Rua said, "This is a priest from Romagna who has come to stay with Don Bosco." The Holy Founder then smiled at me and addressed these words to me, "Yes, you have come to stay with me for a time, perhaps a year, and to see what we do in our boarding schools so that you can go back to your own place and do the same."

I was speechless. Just a few days before leaving Lugo for Alassio, I had gone to confession to the parish priest of the Collegiate Church, Canon Cavina, whom I knew to be better disposed towards religious priests than my ordinary confessor and whom I wished to consult about my vocation. When I had finished my confession I said, "Father, suppose I were to go to Alassio and then to Turin and got the idea of staying with Don Bosco to become a Salesian, what would you say?" The good parish priest answered emphatically, "No, no, you must not stay there. We need priests here. However, you could do this. Stay for a year with Don Bosco, study the way he has succeeded in founding middle and secondary schools in accordance with current laws, then come back here and tell us how it works so we can open the same kind of establishments."

I really did not like the suggestion made by the good priest out of affection for his native place and now, when I had almost forgotten it, Don Bosco's words brought it back to mind. After a moment's hesitation caused by the mysterious revelation of the secret, I hastened to object, "No, I have really come to stay with you forever, if you will have me."

"Well," he said, "at the moment we see each other by the light of this lamp, but tomorrow we will see each other by the light of the sun, and we will get to know one another. So, you are a newly ordained priest? Tomorrow morning you will say the Community Mass for our missionaries who are about to leave for Argentina." I tried to excuse myself since I had only been ordained a month and I was afraid I would become confused if there were many Communions. He answered, "There will be Communions, all right, but you will be able to distribute them very well."

When supper was over, he wished me good night, leaving me with Fr Rua who very kindly led me to what was called the bishop's room, just opposite the rector. He went to get the sheets which be brought back on his shoulder and even set about making my bed. All my attempts to object were in vain. Smiling be said, "We can both help since we are both thin and agile."

Finally, when he finished, he gave me a valuable lesson that I have always remembered as my first *Good Night* received from the great servant of God. A porcelain medallion hung above the bed beside the holy water fount it bore the inscription in gilt letters: 'Whatever God wants is never too much'. Fr Rua invited me to read these beautiful words. Within a few months they would be more profitable to me than I would ever have been able to imagine.

When I was alone, I thought, "This is my resting place, here have I chosen to dwell." I had seen Don Bosco, spoken with him and I had placed myself in his hands. He had read into my past and had even gone so far as to repeat the last words that my good parish priest had spoken to me. He had accepted me into his Congregation and wanted me to celebrate Holy Mass the next morning at the altar of Mary Help of Christians, surrounded by the new missionaries who were going to America. The thought of finding myself in the Oratory of St Francis de Sales, close to the church of Mary Help of Christians, filled me with indescribable consolation and devotion. Don Bosco had also told me that we would see each other "in the light of the sun" on the following day. This, too, made me think that I wanted the sun to rise soon so that I could see the altar of Mary Help of Christians and Don Bosco in the midst of his boys and his spiritual sons, among whom I now found myself. These were the sentiments and impressions that went through my mind on that night and became even more vivid in the heavenly light of my first unforgettable day at the Oratory.

Chapter 2

In the Light of the Sun

Don Bosco had told me, "Tomorrow we shall see each other in the light of the sun." What did he mean? 1t was certainly not only the sun that gives material light; he was undoubtedly speaking of a light that was to illumine my spirit, that light which shone so brightly upon himself. This was how we were to see each other at the altar of our Sacramental Lord and of Mary Help of Christians.

I rose early but remained in my room until dawn filled the Oratory playground with its light. I was not yet acquainted with the house and still had to find my way to the church. As soon as I noticed that the Oratory was astir, I went down and made my way to the door of the sacristy where I found Don Bosco sitting in the midst of his sons hearing confessions. There were priests, clerics and lay brothers present. I recognised among them some of the missionaries who were receiving advice for the last time and hearing the motivating word that would guide them in their challenging apostolate. There were also many altar boys already vested for Mass gathered around the throne of charity and mercy. I, too, would have liked to hear Don Bosco's words, but how was I to do this? He was already besieged, so having made some preparation for Holy Mass, I began to vest.

Two missionary clerics, Evasio Ribagliatti and Giovanni Gisalbertis, served my Mass. There were also many altar servers, whom I believed to be among the clerics of the Oratory. I was greatly edified by the order and precision of their movements and by their diligence in performing the sacred ceremonies. It seemed that I was surrounded by a choir of angels as I left the altar. Even more numerous was the choir of singers around the organ in the gallery. Our entrance into the sanctuary was accompanied by sweet, harmonious music and singing. Then the Congregation of 800 boys began to say their prayers devoutly.   Upon reaching the foot of the altar, I got my first glimpse of the miraculous picture of Mary Help of Christians surrounded by the band of apostles. I was accompanied by the new missionaries who stood in a double line to assist at the Holy Sacrifice of the Mass. I no longer knew what world I was in. I had to make an effort to restrain my tears. My emotion was so strong that I could scarcely celebrate. After my first Mass, this was certainly the most solemn and devout for me.

The times of Consecration and Communion were heavenly moments. Hearing those sweet voices and the angelic hymns sung by the choir and the whole Congregation, seeing so many devout boys approaching the Eucharistic banquet, recalling the many miracles that had contributed towards the building of the church and even more so to the founding of the Congregation and the formation of that band of Salesians already going throughout the world, all filled me with emotion. I was beside myself with joy and I realised at that moment that I was a Salesian and a missionary of Don Bosco and of Mary Help of Christians. Not only was I seeing Don Bosco "in the light the sun", but I was experiencing the heat of those burning rays that emanated from the altar during the celebration of the divine Sacrifice. This was my Mount Tabor, on which I wholeheartedly said to Jesus and Mary what I would have later said with much feeling to Don Bosco, "It is good for us to be here."

Notwithstanding the activities and the hundred and one concerns of that day, Fr Rua did not lose sight of me. He came to the sacristy after Mass to invite me to go for coffee. Sensing my emotion, he very gradually initiated me into Oratory life. He introduced me to many priests but chose to entrust me in a particular way to Fr Lemoyne, whom I greatly esteemed and admired because of his publications in the *Letture Cattoliche*. He was my first guide and from him I received my initial explanations on the running of the Oratory and the Salesian works of which (even though I was unaware at the time of the fact) he was the faithful archivist and historian.

Because of the confidence he inspired in me, I gave in to a secret complacency in showing him how well I knew about Salesian matters. Therefore, I told him all I knew about his writings and those of other Salesians. I also mentioned the *Letture Cattoliche* and the *Biblioteca della Gioventù Italiana* which were familiar to many of my confrères in and outside of the seminary. I expressed my admiration at what I had heard about Don Bosco's cherished idea of setting up a group of ecclesiastic and lay writers who would use his easy style which was within the reach of all. They would write pamphlets on apologetics and Church history for a better moral and religious instruction or young people and adults, particularly on matters concerning current problems. Fr Lemoyne encouraged this innocent conversation of mine while I continued to form a clearer and more complete idea of Don Bosco and his works.

However, since it would have been very inconsiderate to take time from this dear Salesian, I tried to free him from the duty of looking after me that had been assigned to him by Fr Rua. Not wanting to leave me alone, he was kind enough to entrust me to another excellent confrère, Fr Cipriano, who showed me around the Oratory, bookstore, workrooms, classrooms, festive oratory, the little church of St Francis de Sales and so on, giving the appropriate explanations so that I could understand the nature of the establishment. This tour completed Fr Lemoyne's theoretical and historical observations. It was then time for dinner.

Even now I still cannot explain the cordiality of Fr Rua himself who watched over everything and everyone and made all the arrangements in the name of Don Bosco and yet on my arrival at the Oratory he showed me almost preferential treatment. Such privileges and affection bestowed upon a poor priest, with delicate health coming to knock at the door for the first time, must be attributed to the generous, charitable sense of hospitality that prevailed in the Oratory and in the fortunate people who lived there. I was amazed to see everyone around me, including Don Bosco, smiling at me. They looked at me and came to meet me as friends and brothers; we seemed to be old friends already. From the very outset, I was astonished by such kindly behaviour and treatment. I later discovered that it was the same with the boys, especially those newly arrived. I realised that the Oratory was a large home with doors that were always open and where hearts were even more so. It began to dawn on me that I was not as expansive or communicative as all these Salesians. In fact, a few days later when, on Fr Rua's instructions, I was taken to the prefect, Fr Bologna to have my name inscribed in the register or list of the house, and to give information about my home, parents and age, and when I said that I was not yet 23, he looked me in the eye and said, "Then how can you be so serious?" This remark uttered in a half-joking manner, made me reflect on the Salesian attitude that I would have to acquire in look, words and manner if I were to assume a Salesian appearance and be a true son of Don Bosco. I was then approached by Fr Lazzero who joked with me in a friendly fashion. Fr Barberis who was cheerfully conversing with Don Bosco on the evening of my arrival kept my spirits high by telling me jokes. Both Fr Ghivarello who sat opposite me at table and Fr Branda who sat beside me, were always smiling. In short, I was convinced that cheerfulness and cordiality distinguished the sons of the Oratory, and that I was living in the house and in the company of cheerful people and that "serve the Lord in joy" was one of Don Bosco's secrets. Indeed, he would often say, "Rejoice, do good and let the sparrows sing." I, too, therefore, accepted this wonderful plan of action that became clearer and clearer to me "in the light of the sun". However, there was still much more to be seen.

Chapter 3

Missionary Departure

There was a special reason for the cheerfulness which animated Don Bosco's sons that day. The second missionary expedition was about to take place. The missionaries were divided into two groups, one heading to Buenos Aires, capital of Argentina, led by Fr Francesco Bodrato, and the other for Montevideo, capital of Uruguay, led by Fr Luigi Lasagna. Both of these priests were from Alassio and in addition to bringing Don Bosco's educational system to the two American countries, they also brought with them their classical studies that they had completed under the direction of Fr Cerruti. There were ten Salesians in the first expedition; the second had more than twenty. Don Bosco did not shrink from expense or sacrifice where his missions were concerned. He sent the best he had because, sure of the results, he hoped for abundant fruit.

I had seen the missionaries that morning assembled in the sanctuary around Our Lady Help of Christians. We were now united at table with Don Bosco in our midst. He sat between the two missionary leaders, Fr Bodrato on his right and Fr Lasagna on his left. The Greek scholar, Pechenino, sat opposite him and I was to the right of Pechenino, opposite Fr Lasagna and with dear Fr Stefano Bourlot on my left. I was quite moved at finding myself so near to Don Bosco, under his loving glance, and also listening to his gentle, fatherly conversation. Fr Lasagna was the first to speak with me since he had taught my brother Ernesto and spoke about this familiarly. I then entered into conversation with Fr Bourlot who told me about the origins of his missionary vocation. He had felt such a strong call to the foreign missions that if he had not joined the Salesians, his educators, he would have gone to France to enter among the Lazarists. The result of these friendly conversations was a re-awakening within me of the same enthusiasm for the missions and the missionaries, among whom I was already counting myself. There, in the "breaking of the bread" with the sharing of truly Salesian sentiments and ideals, I longed to be part of their labour and sacrifices.

The previous year's impressive farewell ceremony for the missionaries when Fr Cagliero and his companions set out for Argentina was repeated. It took place on the evening of this memorable day in the church of Mary Help of Christians before the miraculous picture of Our Lady surrounded by the twelve apostles. She was carrying Jesus who, with open arms, seemed to invite all to draw near so that he could give himself to them. The church was packed. Cooperators had come from far and wide to witness the event of the generous young sons of Don Bosco who were embarking upon this apostolic enterprise for evangelisation. The Oratory boys and representatives from other schools who recognised rectors, teachers and even companions among the missionaries participated with lively interest.

After hymns, in keeping with the occasion, had been sung, Don Bosco went up to the pulpit to speak about the ceremony. "It was Our Lord himself," he said, "who instituted this ceremony when he sent his apostles all over the world saying: 'Go therefore and make disciples of all nation'. Just as Jesus had received that mission from his Eternal Father and sent the first apostles by his power and in his name, so he entrusted the same mission to these apostles and their successors, his Vicar on Earth and the bishops, the sending of new apostles or missionaries to all people. So it is that the Holy Father and the bishops of the Church, besides assigning lands to be evangelised, also give their mandate and blessing to new expeditions of missionaries who are commissioned to seek and catechise others, leading them to the fold of Jesus Christ or bringing back those who have strayed." Don Bosco then went on to give the results of the previous expedition. Those ten Salesians had already founded a school in San Nicolas de los Arroyos on the Paraná River in Argentina and they were in charge of the *Mater Misericordiae* church for the Italian community in Buenos Aires. They had the responsibility for the large, challenging parish of St John the Evangelist in Boca, an extensive neighbourhood in the capital, populated entirely by Italians, who were almost all from Genoa. They were about to open the first professional school there for orphaned and neglected boys. Therefore, they had opened four houses in the Argentinean Republic in one year. Meanwhile, at Villa Colon near Montevideo, in the Republic of Uruguay, they had opened a school for children of well-to-do families with the intention of entrusting it to a group of the new missionaries. However, the evangelisation of Patagonia continued to be uppermost in his thoughts.

At the conclusion of this report, Don Bosco tenderly thanked Our Lady Help of Christians who had interceded with her Divine Son, Jesus, for so much help, so many graces and blessings on behalf of a very difficult work. This work was undertaken with a shortage of personnel and means but was done in her name and with complete confidence in her maternal goodness. He prayed to his dear Madonna to spread her mantle over these other sons who were about to set out for the same mission. He thanked cooperators and friends for the help they had given and even more for the prayers they had offered. He exhorted all to continue and to increase their efforts in cultivating vocations so that apostolic expeditions, such as this one, might take place annually. In conclusion, he addressed his dear departing sons, bidding them a fatherly goodbye and leaving them with his warm recommendations. They were to seek souls, seek them with zeal and charity and inspire love for Jesus in the Blessed Sacrament and Mary Help of Christians wherever they went.

We were all deeply moved. We looked at the altar, admired the picture of Mary Help of Christians, radiant with its many lights and we were inspired with heavenly thoughts. We saw Don Bosco, so full of emotion and tenderness at this affectionate farewell. Before us were the young priests, clerics and coadjutors, so fervent and resolute at this solemn moment when after a first farewell to the world at their religious profession, they now bid a second one to their families, country and friends, all for the love of Jesus and those redeemed by him.

Monsignor Anglesio, rector of the Little House of Divine Providence and successor of Blessed Cottolengo, imparted the Benediction of the Blessed Sacrament after a solemn singing of the *Tantum Ergo*. Don Bosco then blessed the crucifixes for the missionaries and distributed them with the accompanying gift of his loving words. Here is the treasure which the missionary clasps to his heart, the emblem of his divine mission. Here is the shield and symbol with which he goes out to fight enemy forces, spreading the doctrine and grace of the Redemption. Each one reverently kissed the sacred symbol, placed it around his neck and pressed it to his heart as his only treasure.

Meanwhile, Don Bosco knelt before the altar with all the Superiors and recited prayers for the *itinerarium clericorum*. The missionaries then rose and walked in single file towards Don Bosco and each member of the General Council to whom they bade farewell with a Christian embrace. What sublime lessons were to be learned from that paternal and filial act. Tears of indescribable emotion and noble envy were shed. I, too, was in floods of tears. Yet, amid the general weeping, all the beauty and grandeur of the Salesian apostolate was deeply felt. As the missionaries left the sanctuary and crossed the church, people thronged around to see them and hear a word, a recommendation, a greeting that was, in many cases, a counsel and an invitation for those who remained. With affection and prayer, we accompanied these men who had been chosen by God, while our desire to follow them increased.

Chapter 4

The *Alter Ego* of Blessed Don Bosco

Don Bosco left the Oratory for a few days so that he could accompany his dear missionaries. Fr Rua, however, who never lost sight of new arrivals nor left them alone, kindly called me to his room the next day and began to sound out my dispositions and intentions. I placed myself in his hands and begged him to address me in the more familiar second person and to treat me like any other son of the Oratory. He accepted me under his direction, and we spoke about studies, the education I had received in the seminary, my vocation and certain difficulties that had to be smoothed out with my father for my own peace of mind. He listened for a while and then asked me point blank:

— *Is your writing good?*

— *Reasonably so,* I answered.

— *All right then, give me a sample and if it is reasonably clear, I'll take you on as my secretary.*

— *That's too good of you, Fr Rua, and too much of an honour for me. What shall I write? A thought perhaps?*

— *I'll dictate something to you. Write: 'No one who puts a hand to the plough and looks back is fit for the kingdom of God.'*

— *I think I've understood the first lesson well,* I said, looking up after I had written. *I hope with the help of God to remain faithful and to persevere in my vocation.*

— *Good. You will stay with me and will be my secretary. I will give you work, and we shall get to know each other.*

From that day forward I placed myself wholeheartedly at the disposal of my dear guide who was like a father to me. Oh, what beautiful things I learned at his school of pity, charity and Salesian activity.

Yes, his was truly a school of every virtue. It was a place of doctrine and holiness, but it was first and foremost a school of Salesian formation. Each day I was more and more edified by Fr Rua's punctuality, untiring constancy, religious perfection and self-denial coupled with great gentleness. He had such great charity and refinement in initiating a collaborator in the task he wished to entrust to him. He had prudent concern and insight in getting to know and discern one's aptitudes so as to form them into useful instruments for Don Bosco's work!

Wise Fr Rua, of course, thoroughly studied his secretaries (and he had many), with the view of finding the ways of preparing them for different roles, especially that of prefect or bursar, a responsibility that he himself exercised for the whole Congregation. Indeed, he had a collection of pamphlets or manuals containing or demonstrating the system and method of registration that was suited to the needs of our houses: Mass and stipend registers, bookkeeping and school fees, handbooks for every department in the house and for all internal and external business. He patiently explained their use and with wonderful clarity directed subordinates in making entries and relative notes and showed the importance of the same.

Always exact in keeping up with daily correspondence, he would jot down marginal notes in the letters and then distribute them among us, his secretaries, to answer and present for his signature.

He prepared a good number of such letters for us in the morning and afternoon. Sometimes they had notes inserted by Don Bosco who left it to Fr Rua's judgement to deal with purchases, free admission for boys, acknowledgements for offerings and applications from candidates. I would reply in accordance with the marginal notes, considering myself fortunate to be able to interpret the mind and sentiments of these priests and to imitate that concise, kindly and essential style that I saw as a mark of the Salesian. Thus, Fr Rua studied me to prepare me for the duties of my vocation, but I, too, studied him and in him Don Bosco whose faithful interpreter and living portrait he seemed to be in every aspect of his conduct.

I can truthfully say that Fr Rua's room and office was my well-positioned observatory from where I could see all the characteristics of the life of the Salesian Society. It was like the deck of a great ship whose captain carefully attended to the tiller in order to avoid the reefs and head for the harbour in safety, while at the same time issuing orders for the well-being of all his passengers. It was at Alassio that I had formed a correct idea of a Salesian house that was well-directed and in perfect running order. Now, with Fr Rua I was forming an idea of the grandeur and beauty of everything regarding the Congregation and work of Don Bosco. I therefore considered myself to be very fortunate and thank Our Lady Help of Christians for it with all my heart.

Chapter 5

My Novitiate

At the beginning I still did not know in what my novitiate or time of probation was to consist. Fr Rua, however, put me in touch with Fr Barberis with whom I began the study of the Rule participating in his weekly conference and joining in the recreation of the novices whose playground was separate. However, it was the conferences that interested me most. Interweaving facts and examples about Don Bosco and the history of the Oratory, Fr Barberis gave us a taste for that typically Salesian life of piety and religious observance.

This was the first completely regular year for the novitiate. There was great enthusiasm fostered by a strong desire to become missionaries. I saw in action in my duties with Fr Rua, what Fr Barberis told us in the conferences. The former explained the theory; the latter taught me the practice.

Fr Rua's office was a place of piety and prayer. As soon as we arrived, he would devoutly recite the *actiones* and a Hail Mary and then read a short thought from St Francis de Sales. We would conclude in the same way, i.e., reading a maxim from our saint and saying the *agimus* and a Hail Mary. Even the work was interspersed and seasoned with uplifting sentiments and sayings, since all the marginal notes written by Don Bosco and Fr Rua that we were to use in replying were incentives to faith and confidence in God and Mary Most Holy. They were truly an encouragement to pray, to be resigned, to accept everything from the hand of God, to rest in the Divine Goodness. They consoled, cheered, advised, promised prayers and assured the prayers of the boys and the blessing of Don Bosco. Frequently, opinions and suggestions about vocations were given and the conditions for acceptance of candidates or Sons of Mary were stated. More often, the correspondence concerned cooperators or devotees of Mary Help of Christians who asked for graces and/or sent offerings in thanksgiving for favours received. It was a real apostolate of piety and charity that was being exercised. While at the same time, the general direction of all Don Bosco's work was being implemented.

That room was also visited by priests, rectors and cooperators of every kind and also by the boys. Unless the subject of the discussion was confidential, the secretary also listened to the visitors gaining a more complete idea of the internal and external workings of the Oratory, learning how to seek the glory of God and the good of souls in everything.

Fr Rua had also shown me where it was best to go for community prayers. "It will be good for yourself and for others," he said, "if you always go to the same place in church."

Having read in the Rule that the Salesians should, from time to time, confer with their director and Father on spiritual matters, I asked Fr Rua with whom I could have my private talk. He answered:

— *You should go to Don Bosco, but he is very busy, and you would have to wait a long time. If you would like to speak with me, I am here for you.*

— *I am prepared,* I said.

— *Then get your hat and we'll go to Valsalice where I must hear the young boarders' confessions since today is Saturday. We can talk on the way.*

While we were on our way, he asked his first question:

— *Tell me first of all what it was that made a good impression on you since you came to the Oratory. Then share with me the difficulties you met with and the things you have not enjoyed.*

— *What I most admired,* I answered at once, *both in Alassio and at the Oratory, was seeing the holiness of Don Bosco and finding how all were so united with him. I would even go so far as to say that they were so like him in demeanour; actions and dealings that I saw the spirit of the Founder and Father manifested in and through all.*

— *You are right, my son. This unity in thought, affection and method comes from the family-like education that Don Bosco has given us, winning our hearts and imprinting his ideal upon them. Now, then, if you have anything else pleasant or unpleasant, tell me about it.*

— *I found everything edifying. Among other things, my attention was drawn to the wonderful group of boys who surrounded the altar of Mary Help of Christians on feast days, the choir that seemed to be composed of the angels of heaven, the band that brought joy to solemn school hours. I was especially pleased by the Sodalities of St Aloysius, St Joseph and the Blessed Sacrament. In addition to giving each other good example and exercising a healthy influence over their companions, they promoted spontaneous piety and inspired morality. I would now like to tell you something in confidence. While I was studying theology in Romagna one day, the Professor of Canon Law digressed to speak on the apostolate of St Philip Neri in Rome. One of us who had heard of Don Bosco interrupted and said, "They say that there is a priest in Turin called Don Bosco who has the same type of apostolate in that city, and they are calling him the new St Philip." The famous jurist looked disdainfully at the person who had interrupted and replied, "What can you expect from a poor priest who is surrounded by a gang of hooligans he has picked up from the streets educating them by means of espionage?" We looked at one another and were greatly saddened and scandalised. At the end of the lecture, we hastened to the room of the spiritual director Fr Taroni and we explained what had happened. The good director put his hands to his head and said, "You see how the world judges the Saints? And to think, they used to say the same thing about St Philip." We then heard the explanation. A certain former cleric had come to Turin far military service and while there he attended the Sunday oratory. Since he did not behave properly, he was reprimanded, something that annoyed him intensely. When he returned to his own town, he went from church to church approaching seminarians to give vent to his resentment, saying that there were spies at the Oratory.*

— These observations that you have made on Don Bosco's system will be useful to you.

That was how my first private talk came to an end.

Chapter 6

A Two-Hour Conversation with Don Bosco

Don Bosco finally returned. Anxious to speak with him and make myself known "in the light of the sun", I made an immensely satisfying confession to him and then obtained the longed-for grace of a whole afternoon with him. These were two beautiful hours of conversation during which all the most interesting facets of my vocation were brought to light.

I told him that I was not strong physically. I informed him about the studies I had completed during my three years with the Benedictines at Cesena and my seven years at the seminary in Faenza. In short, I tried to place myself in his hands.

Don Bosco began by explaining his Preventive System of pure and patient charity and spoke about gentleness and great friendliness with everyone. He told me about three boys who had to be sent away from the Oratory because of bad behaviour. They wanted to come to Don Bosco's room one by one to acknowledge that they were unworthy to stay at the school. They asked to make their confession to him so that they could go with their Father's forgiveness. He promised to help them always and encouraged them to keep their good resolutions and not to lose contact with him.

He then expressed his desire to entrust to me the first fifteen Sons of Mary who were already at the Oratory in the first year of the institution of this work. He explained the method to be followed for logical analysis and composition and the running of what was then called the 'School of Fire' both because of the shortness of the course as its members were adults and because of the fervour with which these good sons dedicated themselves to the study of Latin.

He offered me Latin phrases to be analysed logically, then gave me a sentence to be divided into phrases, recommending in conclusion that I do many, many exercises.

Like a good native of Romagna, I tried to suggest to Don Bosco the need for a foundation at Bologna, our metropolis, pointing out the timeliness of such a foundation. I said that the Catholic Youth Organisation had then been established and had formed members who were ready to fight for Catholic institutions and in the defence of priests. Don Bosco let me continue speaking and then calmly replied, "We do not have this fiery spirit of combat. We do not meddle in politics; we aim only at working among young people and pray to be left in peace in this work. If we were to be invited or summoned to something other than our mission among boys, we would not go because this would not be our place." It must also be noted that I had spoken just as the natives of Romagna speak in certain cases, i.e., in a hot, warlike manner.[1]

I had made a bad start! I then told Don Bosco the reason for my presence at the Oratory, almost without realising that I was doing so.

— *Do you know what brought me here? I said Dominic Savio!*
— *How? Asked Don Bosco.*
— *Here is my story. When I was nine years old, my good parents sent me to school with the Benedictine Monks of Santa Maria del Monte near Cesana where I seriously and diligently prepared for my First Holy Communion made on June 1, 1863. I had an aunt on my father's side who was a Benedictine nun in the same city and her convent was famous because it was there that the mother of Pius VII became a nun. She was buried there and upon his return from exile, the Pope visited her grave. As a present for my First Holy Communion, this aunt gave me a copy of the 'Life of Dominic Savio' that you had recently published. I read it with great interest and wrote beneath the picture of the pious boy: 'May I be able to follow you'. Then, because of the suppression of religious orders in 1866, we were all sent home. A short time later, I entered the seminary of Faenza where a companion of mine, who was*

---

1   During those catastrophic times, the Catholic Youth Organisation had to react against the sects that were suffocating all religious freedom. Since the members of the government were also sectarians, the religious struggles soon began to look like political competitions. Don Bosco responded with his Sunday oratorios, with the Christian education of young people and with all the means offered by the press, but he never considered it part of his mission to fight or in any way to answer violence with violence.

somewhat opinionated, asked me for a book to read during rest period. I told him that he had already borrowed all my interesting books and that I only a few lives of the saints left, and I didn't think they would appeal to a poetic, imaginative and rather fashionable person like himself. "Give me anything, anything. I want to read, not to sleep." I went to my room and crossed out my prayer to Dominic Savio to spare myself the teasing of that fellow (cowardice, I admit), and I gave him the book. Twelve years have passed since that time, and the saintly boy, remembering my petition, has granted that confused desire that came from reading about his life towards the end of Mary's month and the day of my First Holy Communion.

When I was finished, Don Bosco smiled and said, "If ever the 'Life of Dominic Savio' is reprinted, I would like you to insert this grace that you have received, adding it to the others already found there." I did, in fact, send an account of it from America, but I do not know whether or not it was published. However, I can testify that this was the desire that our blessed father expressed to me.

The conversation did not end there. I asked, perhaps somewhat imprudently, if there were any imitators and followers or Dominic Savio's holiness among our companions, pupils or clerics. With amiable simplicity and visible pleasure, the Blessed Founder first quoted the former companions of Dominic Savio. Don Bosco assured me that, as a boy, Fr Cerruti had had such a horror of sin that he fainted at the mere mention or it. He added, that once, he preached on the disbelief of Thomas who would not believe in the resurrection of Jesus. He was explaining to the boys that when he commits sin, he denies the Passion, Death and Resurrection of Jesus. At that point he saw Cerruti grow sorrowful and faint. He also spoke of Fr Bonetti. "I would have beautiful things to say about him if I were to write his life!" He then spoke of the boys who had recently donned the clerical habit and named Edward MacKiernan, the Irish boy who, he assured me, was another St Aloysius Gonzaga. When I later heard that MacKiernan had been sent as rector to London, the place of our angelic boy's vision, I could not fail to link this fact with Don Bosco's words. He mentioned other names, but I will not divulge them since the people are still living and it would not do to offend or tempt their modesty in accordance with the admonition of the Holy Spirit "praise only after death".

Don Bosco took great pleasure in speaking about his boys and spiritual sons and he had good reason for doing so.

Bishop Pedro de Lacerda, Bishop of Rio de Janeiro in Brazil, came to the Oratory that year. A few years later, he told me that at the time he not only wanted to consult Don Bosco about his personal doubts and difficulties of conscience, but also wanted to hear the opinion of the best boys in the house. He therefore made the same request of Don Bosco as I had made, adding, "I want you to call five of your boys who are faithful imitators of Dominic Savio because I want them to rid me of certain fears about my responsibilities before God." Don Bosco sent for five boys who serenely and respectfully faced the bishop while with Don Bosco, and they were open and frank. The latter introduced them to the bishop with the following words: "This American bishop wants to question you to find out what you think about certain cases that he will reveal to you. Speak as freely with him as you would with me."

Don Bosco then left, leaving one boy with the bishop and taking the others to wait in another room. The bishop then made his condition known to the boy who had remained with him. He was in an immense city with almost a million people whose salvation weighed heavily on his conscience. The devil and his ministers, sects, Protestantism and every vice were leading people to hell every day. Even he, the bishop, had been stoned while preaching from his pulpit. He had few priests, and some of those were not fulfilling their duties, so he had come to ask Don Bosco for priests. Given his responsibility, would he not have to answer for the loss of so many people? Could he be saved? The boy, terrified and almost dumbstruck at so horrible and disconcerting a picture replied at once and assured him that he could be saved. The very fact that he had come so far to ask Don Bosco for priests showed the great care he had for these people. The bishop answered with these words, "Very well, pray to Mary Help of Christians, to Dominic Savio, your good companion, that Don Bosco may give me good missionaries. And would you also like to come and help me to save those poor people?"

"Oh yes," came the answer, "I will ask Don Bosco to prepare me well and then I hope that I, too, will become a good missionary."

"We'll see each other again, then." The same took place with the other boys.

"They all absolved me," said the pious prelate, "from all fault and freed me from the great weight of my responsibility with regard to those people, promising to pray that Don Bosco would send his missionaries to Brazil very soon." Alluding to this in a song dedicated to Bishop Pedro de Lacerda, Fr Lemoyne described the miraculous catch of fish that Simon Peter was unable to cope with because of its weight, and so he called fishermen from John's boat to come to his aid and was then able to take in a most abundant catch of fish.

Chapter 7

Don Bosco's Dreams

Another beautiful coincidence took place to complete the grace worked in me by Dominic Savio. It increased my perception of Don Bosco's holiness and his work of salvation and renewal among the young people, a work to be performed all over the world.

One evening towards the end of November, we were at supper. I was opposite Fr Ghivarello and next to Fr Branda at Don Bosco's table. Fr Ghivarello whispered to Fr Branda, "Don Bosco is going to tell us about a dream at the Good Night." Hearing news that was unfamiliar to me, I looked at the two priests in amazement. "What? Don Bosco is going to tell us a dream?"

"Yes," they said, "Don Bosco is going to tell us about one of his dreams."

I paused and thought, *What's the use of coming to this house to hear about dreams?* Seeing my perplexity, Fr Ghivarello said, "Don't you know about Don Bosco's dreams?"

"No, I certainly don't," I answered.

"Oh," he said, "you will learn..."

My mind was filled with what was to come. Even before leaving the refectory, we heard that all the boys of the house, students and artisans and the entire personnel of the Oratory, in all about a thousand people, had gathered under the portico. Prayers were said with a special, almost supernatural devotion. Big and small, all wanted to hear about Don Bosco's dream.

After a brief examination of conscience, at the end of prayers, all stood. A thunderous applause greeted Don Bosco who appeared in the midst of the boys with outstretched hands. He made his way to the platform near a pillar outside the refectory door. The boys took hold of their Father and lifted him up to the platform. Don Bosco smiled, stretched out his hands again and signalled that he was about to speak. There was perfect silence as he began to relate his beautiful dream about Dominic Savio.

In this dream, Savio appeared in white garments with a band of prayerful, virtuous pupils of the Oratory. In sweetest song he explained and prophesied the trouble the Church would experience at the approaching death of Pius IX. [He also spoke of the difficulties] the Oratory would experience, including the death of six boys, and two others dear to Don Bosco's heart. He then offered Don Bosco a bouquet of flowers representing the virtues that he should have his pupils practise. Finally, he showed him three pages on which the pupils had been categorised as innocent, reformed and hardened in sin. Don Bosco's horror at seeing this third page was such that he uttered a cry and fainted. Fr Lemoyne, who was in the adjoining room, hastened in and arrived just in time to catch him. For many days, Don Bosco had not been able to free himself from this agonising impression. He used the revelation, however, to tell the rector at Lanzo the names of the boys to be sent away, even though under all appearances they seemed to be worthy pupils of the school.

That evening, another priest and I were taking a walk when we met Don Bosco whom I questioned shyly, but with great interest. "Who are the two people dear to your heart who are to die this year?"

He answered: "Who else but the two?" He said this with a smile to avoid the question. I know that my companion went to confession to ask where he was on the pages that Savio had shown him, and our good Father made certain revelations that gave him food for thought.

After that dream, the Officer for Public Safety at Borgo Dora, Angelo Piccono, having heard about Don Bosco's prophetic announcement concerning the death of eight people, wanted to be informed of how things had turned out. His wish was granted. When the prophecy was fulfilled to the letter, he abandoned his career, became a Salesian and was later our companion in the missions, leaving the most pleasant of memories in the houses of Buenos Aires, Montevideo, San Nicolas and Patagonia.

We were with Piccono, then a cleric, when on one occasion we plucked up the courage to ask Don Bosco some questions about his extraordinary dreams and gifts. I had been asked by my seminary rector, Fr Taroni, to write to him every week about anything special that I had seen in Don Bosco, and I was trying to satisfy him. Don Bosco had invited us to have a cup of coffee with him but since the coffeepot was small and there were many guests, someone said, "You had better pour the coffee, Don Bosco, because unless the miracle of the multiplied chestnuts is repeated, there won't be enough for everyone."

Don Bosco smiled and fixed his gaze on us as though it were a serious matter and said, "What do you think poor Don Bosco could do if he did not receive special help from heaven at every moment? I assure you that the correspondence of our boys works miracles."

He then told us about the miracle of the hosts. On one of the most solemn feast days, the sacristan had forgotten to prepare enough hosts far a general Communion, even though he had been reminded to do so. When it was time for the distribution, Don Bosco took the ciborium out of the tabernacle, uncovered it and saw that it contained only about fifteen hosts. He began to give Communion with these to the boys, thinking that when they had been distributed, he could go back to the tabernacle and get more hosts. He went along the altar rail once with Communion, then a second time, and so on without interruption, with new hosts appearing all the time. "I began to tremble and feel confused at the sight of those particles that were increasing in number until I reached the last of the large number of communicants and I still had some hosts left. When I went back to the altar, I discovered that I had been mistaken in thinking that there was another ciborium. I realised that God had wanted to reward so many good boys who would have otherwise missed their Holy Communion and would have been left fainting like the crowds in the desert because of the lack of Divine Grace."

On another occasion, we steered the conversation back to the subject of his dreams since he had digressed on the previous occasion. With filial confidence, we asked Don Bosco what we should think of them especially because it seemed that they contained mysterious warnings and prophetic announcements. He gave us a similar answer. He would have been powerless to assist, guide and attract so many boys to God without means and personnel if Mary Help of Christians, who had entrusted that mission to him, had not come to his aid with enlightenment and abundant material and spiritual assistance.

The beautiful, practical lesson that Blessed Don Bosco gave us bound us closer to him and inspired us with confidence in God and Mary Most Holy. They strengthened us in our vocation, preparing us for those duties that our good Father would later entrust to us.

Chapter 8

From Novice to Professed

Meanwhile, I was continuing my occupations in Fr Rua's office and making the practices of piety with the novice clerics under the guidance of Fr Barberis. The latter continued to give us his very practical conferences filled with the Salesian spirit and always illustrated with examples from the life of Don Bosco and the dreams relating to the origin and development of the Congregation. It is easy to understand why I regretted having to discontinue my attendance at these conferences since I was already a priest and also because Don Bosco availed himself of the privileges granted to him by Pius IX who esteemed and loved him very much, and I was admitted to vows at Christmas. However, I continued to listen to those conferences from behind the door. Later, when I was in America, I begged Fr Barberis not to do to others what he had done to me, i.e., to exclude anyone from the conferences just because they were already priests.

Christmas and the time of my profession were fast approaching. One day after lunch, Don Bosco turned to me and another priest, chaplain of the Holy House of Loreto, to tell us in a very kindly way that we were to be deacon and subdeacon at the Holy Mass that he would celebrate as usual on Christmas night. I was to be subdeacon and, beside myself with joy, thanked Don Bosco for my good fortune. I also told my companion who had been chosen as deacon that we could truly deem ourselves lucky to be able to take our places beside a saint in the Divine Sacrifice. This companion, however, with the greatest indifference answered me, "I am not accepting; I don't feel like it." Well, I thought to myself, it seems that he is not one of us! In fact, he was so undecided about his Salesian vocation that he kept his trunk in the entrance and soon he returned home. I obtained the grace, therefore, of serving as deacon at the solemn midnight Mass, where I was imbued with the holy dispositions of Don

Bosco so that I was able to share more abundantly in the infinite fruits of the Holy Sacrifice.

Thus, began the day of December 25, 1876, the day of my perpetual profession that I made in the hands of our Blessed Founder. There were seven of us priests who made our profession, and our good Father gave us a masterly conference for the occasion, explaining the whole of our religious life in a very gracious light.

He began by reminding us of the simple, famous programme that he usually offered when inviting adults to join the Congregation, "Don Bosco promises and assures you of three things: bread, work and heaven." He then set out to give us a detailed explanation of the subject of which he was speaking. He told us that as his professed sons, he would be taking us by the hand and acting as the guide who would introduce us into the Salesian house, i.e., the Congregation. It would be enough for him, he said, to take us on a tour of the whole Oratory or Motherhouse because we would find its image and likeness in all the houses.

He then began to give us a virtual tour. He took us to the entrance where we were graciously welcomed by the Salesian doorkeeper whom Don Bosco defined as a great treasury for a house. He also introduced us to the prefect, showed us the rector's office and described the kindness and fatherliness proper to these roles. He showed us the playgrounds teeming with boys and their assistants, all engaged in various games or cheerful conversations. Then he accompanied us to the classrooms and study halls, explaining how those priests and clerics had a special system or method of leading their pupils to carry out their duties. He made the same statement in the workshops, specifying the duties of the teacher and his assistant. This, he said, is how all Salesians, priests, clerics and coadjutors work with one aim in view, and all of one mind with the same intention of evangelising others.

He then pointed up to his little room at the centre of the Oratory where he invited us to visit him often, to tell him of our impressions so that he could help us to resolve our difficulties and could speak to us as a friend.

After this, he went down to the refectories, where with simple, fatherly tenderness he told us to taste the bread of Don Bosco, bread that he called providential because it was paid for by the charity of so many good cooperators, and bread that we would share with our poor boys, students and artisans.

The next place visited was the festive oratory. With him we observed the vast movement of boys and adults who came on Sundays for religious services. We remarked on the organisation of the catechism classics, games, religious practices, and so on. This was the heart of Don Bosco's existence.

After the magnificent exposition of the first two parts of his programme, bread and work, Don Bosco turned to us and said with great pleasure: "After all we have seen, the best still remains, not only to be seen, but to be tasted: heaven. We were in suspense, curious to hear what Don Bosco's heaven was like. It was the beloved church of Mary Help of Christians! He described it to us, having us not only admire it, but even savour and enjoy it as truly heaven on earth. He led us through the door at the entrance and straight up to the picture of his noble Mother, 'Don Bosco's Madonna'. He spoke to us about the solemn functions with his large group of clergy; the devotion that prevailed among the multitude of boys and faithful who sang and listened to the Word of God, proclaimed frequently and with great fervour. He helped us to appreciate the music of his own sons (at that moment it was Fr Cagliero's music) and the harmonious strains of the organ, but most of all, he called our attention to the frequent reception of the sacraments, the constant visits of the confrères and boys to the Blessed Sacrament and to the altar of Mary Help of Christians. Having reached this point, he asked us, "Doesn't all this truly seem like a beautiful prelude to heaven?"

In conclusion he said to us, "You will find these same things in all our Salesian houses and churches. Everywhere you will meet those three elements necessary for our life: bread, work and heaven. In addition, if you should ever find bitter water as happened to the Jews in the desert, I mean displeasures, illness, trials, difficulties or temptations, have recourse to the remedy prescribed by Moses: put in the wood that has the property of making the water sweet, i.e., the wood of the Holy Cross of our Lord Jesus Christ, the memory of his Passion and the Divine Sacrifice renewed on our altars."

Thus, ended the memorable conference on that Christmas, the day of our profession. It lasted an hour and a half, but it passed in a flash, leaving an indelible impression upon our minds.

From the very beginning, I had duties proper to professed members, partly because of the School of Fire, partly because I was working in Fr Rua's office. When Fr Guanella, who had been prefect in the sacristy left, I was also given that task. God had another mission for Fr Guanella, one like that of

Don Bosco. This was precisely why he had come to study Don Bosco and his method for three years and acquire his spirit as he himself said and proved by his outstanding virtue.

I also did some work with Fr Giuseppe Bologna in the prefect's office, answering letters and writing admission certificates. This varied work gave me practical knowledge of the whole Oratory and all of Don Bosco's work.

However, my work did not end there. My Sundays were usually spent at the festive oratory, directed at that time by dear Fr Domenico Milanesio who had also asked to be sent to the missions and shared my hopes and sentiments. I also went to the oratory of St Aloysius where, after the celebration of Holy Mass on the Feast of the Epiphany, I gave my first sermon to the boys, explaining the mystery of the adoration of the Magi and their and our vocation to the faith and love of Jesus our Lord.

Chapter 9

Lessons from Father Rua

In every place and at every moment I received splendid lessons and wonderful examples of Salesian virtue. This fact increased my enthusiasm for my vocation. I must now talk about those lessons and the example given by Fr Rua.

The work he assigned to me was varied and unending, but he also wanted to know how I was getting along in school and to see whether my method was that of Don Bosco. At the end of my first month's teaching, he asked me if I had given my pupils what was called a placement test. I told him that I did not understand what this meant. "Oh," he said, "it is very important. It is one of the typical features of our classes and it is a great incentive for competition. It consists of a weekly essay done in class and another more demanding monthly test summarising the month's work."

I thanked Fr Rua for the guidelines given me and, having decided upon my placement work or test, I handed him the pupils' work. He looked at it and smiled as he said, "This is what the pupils have done, but we must see the teacher's work, too. Mark each one's mistakes, classify each exercise with a grade and make me a list according to merit. In this way I shall be able to praise teacher and pupils." I obeyed him exactly and expressed my gratitude to him for having given me an examination as Don Bosco had already done in logical analysis and composition.

Fr Rua was keenly interested in the formation of the clerics whose school of philosophy and theology was the object of his concern. One day he took a little stool that he had in his room and sat behind the headboard of the bed so that he was not visible to those who came into the room. Then he said to me,

"I am leaving you in charge of the office. I have to give the clerics an exam in theology today and I must prepare for it. If anyone comes, say that I am not here. Look, I really am out of circulation." I promised to do as he asked.

Someone knocked, opened the door and asked: "Is Fr Rua here?"

I answered, "No, he is not."

The visitor came forward rather boldly and asked, "Has he gone out? Where did he go?" I was at a loss as to what to answer and, seeing that I had not succeeded in hiding him, Fr Rua stood up and asked, "What do you want?" He dealt with the questioner very quickly and then said to me, "You see? Both of us have cut a bad figure, you looking like a liar and I looking as though I was hiding to avoid seeing anyone. Therefore, learn to do your part properly. If anyone knocks, do not let him open the door. You open the door just a little and, holding it firmly say, 'Fr Rua is not here now.' Greet them nicely, and then close the door. We shall thus be left in peace, I who have to study, and you who have to work." I learned that lesson well and succeeded magnificently in covering for him who was making such a zealous preparation for our clerics' exam.

He often had to correct us regarding the procedures of liturgical ceremonies. He was very familiar with them but wanted us to learn them from the *Rubricae Missalis*. He would say to me, for example, "Look up the rubrics to find out how you should hold the chalice when approaching or leaving the altar." I seem to remember it saying *ante pectus*. I did so and discovered that this was exactly the way it was, and I realised that I had been holding the chalice too low.

To train me in the management of financial administration he had me make calculations in the different books or registers called handbooks. He wanted me to give him a weekly account of the workshops, sacristy finances, Masses said and those still to be said and so on. He even had me keep an account of how much was spent by each cleric on clothes, shoes and similar items. He used this information to give timely advice on the spirit of poverty and economy. He himself was a model in every sphere of economy such as in the use of paper and pens, lights, journeys, etc.

He prudently prohibited his secretaries from using paper with the letterhead of the Oratory. He said that only official documents of the Congregation or house should bear this stamp.

When I asked him what I should do with the large set of books which had been sent to me from home, he replied, "I shall only tell you what I myself have done with my own books: I have always put them in the common library." I also received a writing support which when placed on the table allowed one to write while standing; as it was rather elegant, he suggested my sending it along to the visitors' room. "For you, as for me," he added, "a chair placed on the table does very well. Try it and you will see that it reaches the chest exactly." Indeed, this turned out to be quite comfortable for me.

One day, a gentleman came into Fr Rua's room. He seemed to know him and Don Bosco well. After an exchange of greetings, the *Cavaliere* (as Fr Rua addressed him) walked across the room behind where I was writing and began to grumble about the Salesians who were tearing down the ancient choir in the church and building another which, he said, looked like the bridge over the River Po. The railing was, in fact, made of iron and it was not yet covered and decorated and so it reminded one of the old iron bridge over the river that has been replaced by a stone bridge. He added that if Don Bosco could afford so many new developments, he no longer needed the help of his cooperators. Fr Rua went on writing as he usually did while listening to people he knew, only raising his eyes now and then and said, "Oh, no, Signor Cavaliere. These works were necessary and were done economically. Later on, you will see how well everything will turn out."

The man persisted, however, walking up and down, and stamping his foot as though he were annoyed. Then he said, "I don't suppose I will be able to see Don Bosco. There are always so many people besieging him! Very well, then pray for me." And taking Fr Rua's hand he left a wad of currency in it and went away.

I was just going to ask who that insolent fellow was, but Fr Rua, looking at me, showed me what was in his hand and said, "Did you hear that man? His bark is worse than his bite. He came to give me alms which we urgently need for today. It adds up to 20,000 Lire. Let us thank Divine Providence for it."

I was astounded to see on the one hand such great simplicity coupled with untiring work, and on the other the extraordinary graces, heavenly enlightenment and bountiful blessings that rained on Don Bosco's work.

I, too, can bear witness to miracles worked at that time by Mary Help of Christians. I would like to tell you one that has a bearing on the subject of this chapter. One day I went to see Don Bosco in his room and after having discussed my personal concerns, he said, "I have a letter here from a priest and fellow countryman of yours, Fr Nenci saying that he, too, would like to come here." I was a bit taken aback and I felt obliged to make known to our blessed Founder that this good priest had already been dismissed from the Jesuit novitiate because of tuberculosis. They had said that his lungs were almost completely destroyed. As a friend I had been present during the light meal that he ate and had seen the care that his family lavished upon him, going to extraordinary expense for remedies and special food. Furthermore, when he gave me back a volume of the Summa of St Thomas that I had lent him, my mother wrenched it from my hand saying, "This has to be disinfected because that good priest, like his brother and sister, has a terrible disease." Don Bosco listened with a smile then said, "I know all about it, but he has great confidence in Mary Help of Christians. By coming here to become a Salesian, he hopes, rather he is firmly convinced, that he will be cured." After he said this, he gave me a closed letter and said, "Here is my reply. Put it in with one of yours and then mail it."

I put the letter in my pocket and upon finding Fr Rua I said to him, "Please listen for a moment and tell me what I should do. Don Bosco handed me a letter that seems to be a letter of acceptance for an excellent priest from my hometown." I explained to him how this priest was in an advanced state of consumption and had no hope of being cured. He had already tried the Jesuit novitiate at Calais when he was still strong but was forced to leave. I asked what he thought and whether I should send the letter or perhaps he would explain to Don Bosco the dangers if a sick man in his condition were to be admitted. Fr Rua looked at me in a very serious, almost scandalised way and answered, "Would you dare to intercept a letter from Don Bosco? Would you dare to oppose the designs that God and Mary Help of Christians may have for that priest whom you believe to be unfit and sick beyond hope? Do you not know that Don Bosco has an understanding with Our Lady?"

I was taken aback by these questions and answered immediately, "Oh, I'm sorry. I had truly looked at the question from another point of view." I went immediately to mail the letter from Don Bosco to Fr Nenci and added a short congratulatory one from me.

I had no sooner departed for America in November 1877, when this priest arrived at the Oratory. Don Bosco, perhaps remembering the difficulties I had raised, wrote, "Fr Nenci is here with us. He is doing well and works with good will with the philosophy and theology clerics. Who knows? Perhaps he will pay you a visit in the American missions." I later learned from the missionaries who had come from Turin that Fr Nenci was teaching a regular class, preached zealously and effectively and had made his triennial vows. It is to be noted, however, that some who had come to Don Bosco in poor health and were subsequently cured and strengthened, forgot that if Don Bosco's Madonna had granted them health, it was because they were to use it in his work. They returned to their cities and families but did not live long. Not only did they not enjoy a lengthy well-being, but they did not even carry out the undertakings they had planned.

One morning, when I was about to tackle the correspondence, Fr Rua approached me with an envelope in his hand and said quite mysteriously, "I have a wonderful work to entrust to you, but you must first put yourself in God's grace and make a good Act of Contrition because Don Bosco's handwriting is difficult to decipher. These are the Regulations of the Houses that have been reviewed, corrected and almost rewritten by him. Now the final draft needs to be printed; therefore, copy them carefully."

It goes without saying that I was very pleased with the precious task, and I applied myself to it diligently. It was an opportune lesson for me to transcribe such an interesting original work that was intended to regulate the roles and activities of all of Don Bosco's work. During that year 1876–77, following the approval of the Rules of the Society and in preparation for the First General Chapter, the houses were in the process of being canonically organised and fundamental norms for the carrying out of every duty were being established. I, therefore, had the good fortune of being in a position to compare theory and practice. I thus formed a complete idea of what a Salesian Community should be by copying word for word what Don Bosco wished not only for his sons in the individual houses, but also for his pupils, students, artisans, boarders and day students. How much good I derived from those pages that I kissed with veneration.

After I finished the work, which I did as a true a labour of love, I presented Don Bosco's manuscript to Fr Rua and with mingled fear and hope I boldly asked for a reward. "Fr Rua," I said rather timidly, "now that I have copied all these pages to the best of my ability, will you do me the favour of letting me keep one of them so I can have an autograph of Don Bosco and keep it as a relic?"

Fr Rua, surprised at my presumption, answered at once, "Whatever are you saying? Don't you know that every scrap of Don Bosco's writing is carefully preserved in the archives of the Congregation? All the more so because this is the code of Salesian life! If I gave you a page of the Regulations, they would be mutilated." He easily convinced me of the impropriety of my request, and I resigned myself to having a copy later on when the Regulations were printed.

Since then, I have admired the beauty, the practicality and the simplicity of the Regulations, a true masterpiece of our holy founder. Above all, and notwithstanding their conciseness, I found every article filled with prayerfulness and charity both in the first part concerning the confrères and in the related second part dealing with the pupils. They were really inspired by the spirit of a genuine family whose members pray, work and keep cheerful, all in peace and charity.

During the same year, 1877, Blessed Don Bosco revised the 'Regulations for the Festive Oratories',[2] two copies of which I was very happy to obtain, the first ones printed by the unforgettable bookbinder Gastini, on the eve of my departure for Argentina. These Regulations with the corresponding registers were useful in the founding of the first festive oratory in Buenos Aires, Almagro, named St Francis de Sales in imitation of the Oratory at Valdocco.

---

2   Based on that published around 1852 Cf. Lemoyne, *Memorie biografiche di Don Bosco*, vol. III, p.91.

Chapter 10

Illness and Miraculous Cure: A Dramatic Intervention

Finally, after repeated colds, persistent coughing throughout the night, exhaustion and high fevers, I was reduced to such a state that I could no longer stand. In the middle of January 1877, I was sent to Alassio to recover since I continually coughed up blood and showed other symptoms that frightened everyone. Upon the advice of the doctor, I returned to Turin on January 25. Halfway through the journey I had a haemorrhage and thus entered the Oratory more dead than alive. The doctor declared that I was beyond any remedy. He could do nothing for me, but my real remedy came from another source.

I had written a letter, almost my last will and testament, to our good Father from Alassio. I thanked him for having accepted me into the Congregation notwithstanding my poor health, my inability to work when there was so much to be done, and the fact that I seemed to be causing nothing but inconvenience wherever I went. Feeling that my end was near, I declared myself happy to die as a Salesian. However, Don Bosco was in Rome and so he only received my letter before the feast of St Francis de Sales, when he returned to the Oratory.

Meanwhile, a further complication set in to make my story even more dramatic. Before making my vows, I had asked Bishop Luigi Tesorieri of Imola, for the *discessit* from the diocese so that I could enter the Salesian Congregation. Instead of sending the permission to me at the Oratory, however, the bishop had sent it to my home in Lugo. I had written home to say that I would be staying with Don Bosco for a year because I wanted to avoid opposition from my father who, though a good Christian, was counting on me for the education of my six younger brothers and sisters. There had been nothing to alarm him in my plan to stay with Don Bosco for a year on the advice of the parish priest because of the desire I had often expressed of furthering my ecclesiastical studies. All my castles came tumbling down when the bishop's *discessit* fell into my father's hands. He summoned all the Latin he had learned from singing the Office of Our Lady, Sunday Vespers and even the lamentations of Holy Week in interpreting that episcopal document that contained the clues to the secret. Fortunately, deeming himself sufficiently well-versed in Latin, he refused to consult any priest!

While on the subject, I would like to relate an incident from my childhood. One day in 1859 my father was at the Lago railway station with the conductor of the band. As the porter tried to load a huge suitcase onto the wagon, it fell to the ground and the owner shouted, "*Bestia et universa pecora!*" The band conductor, wishing to complete the Psalm added "*Serpentes et volucres pennati.*" My father corrected him, "No, no, it's *pennatae.*" I am not writing this to show that he knew about gender and number, but that the three good men, instead of blaspheming, remembered the Office of Our Lady. My father then challenged him to a bet. If it were *pennatae*, the band conductor would have to come and play us a serenade; and it if were *pennati*, father was to treat the local musicians to a barrel of wine. The book of devotions that good Christians at that time often carried in their pockets was solemnly produced and my father claimed victory, but all was kept secret. Then one night, while we little ones were already in bed, the band began to play its serenade below our windows. Mother let us get out of bed so that we could share in the *Latinistic* triumph of our father. There was singing, playing and also a drop of wine. We, too, learned to appreciate the truly pleasant and peaceful celebrations of the good old days.

However, let us return to a more difficult Latin which, in my father's hands was to lead to another kind of music here at the Oratory, close to Don Bosco and of his making.

Everyone at home wanted to have a say in the matter! My older brother said, "Look, father, you invited Fr Cerruti to Giuseppe's first Mass and now he has taken him away." My poor mother, a woman of great faith, had recourse to her confessor, the good canon and parish priest of St James. He was a family friend, but not favourably disposed towards religious vocations. He pronounced his opinion, "Fr Giuseppe has made a great mistake in leaving his family and diocese." By the way, the same priest wrote me a strong letter stating: "And whoever does not provide for relatives, and especially for family members, has denied the faith and is worse than an unbeliever." I had fun answering him, "How did he get it into his head," I asked, "to take me for a widow with children?" I recommended that he should not play with scriptural texts. Meanwhile, there was great dismay and deep affliction at home where there was no one to take my part.

I was bedridden and unable to answer the letters that were piling up around me. However, I felt peaceful and immensely satisfied about my vocation. Don Bosco had told me from the beginning: "Don't worry; it is only a little storm that will soon pass over. You will later experience a great peace and have a magnificent day of brilliant sunshine." I considered these words to be prophetic.

My father thought that there was a secret conspiracy going on about my vocation, so he decided to remove my brothers from Alassio. However, he decided to first come to Turin to hear from me. In reality, he had great respect for me as a priest. He reached the Oratory on the morning of February 4 when the transferred feast of St Francis de Sales was being celebrated. He entered the church of Mary Help of Christians during the community Mass with its prayers, hymns, clergy and general Communion. This was the first step towards appeasing him, almost making him a Salesian. He went to the sacristy and noticed a list on the door containing the names of the priests attached to the church with the signal by which each could be summoned when required. He saw my name at the end of the list with a line running through it. He asked the sacristan why that particular name had been crossed out and was told, "Fr Vespignani is seriously ill. He coughs up blood and it seems that the doctors have given up on him."

My father was very upset and went into the church to pray. He then came out through the main door and went to look for the entrance to the Oratory. Just at that moment a carriage pulled up at the gate, two priests descended and came toward my father who exchanged a few words with the older of the two:

— *Are you coming here to Don Bosco's Oratory?* asked my father.
— *Yes, are you also coming? Do you have a friend or relative here?*
— *Yes, my son, Fr Giuseppe Vespignani is here.*
— *Very good indeed!* he said, taking him by the arm. *We are good friends! Come with me.*

Suddenly the gates opened wide, and a thousand voices were raised to cheer Don Bosco amid the festive notes of the band. Yes, Don Bosco was back from

Rome to spend the feast of the saintly patron of the Congregation in the company of his boys. All ran up, trying to kiss his hand. My father, who was deeply moved, also tried to do so. That kiss dispelled all the clouds, and he, too, became young and a son of that great Father.

Don Bosco introduced him at once to Fr Rua, who greeted him and told him about me in the gentlest possible terms. He offered to accompany him to my room personally, but in the meantime entrusted him to another confrère and had the delicacy to come and warn me. "There is a gentleman at the entrance who has come to visit you. He is rather stout and short and has good colour."

"Oh, is it father? Is he annoyed or angry?"

"No, no, he is in the best possible mood. He met Don Bosco and was very impressed. Everything is fine, don't worry."

We hid everything that might give a less than favourable impression, tidied up the room a bit and then father came into the room smiling. His first words were, "You are in heaven here! If it were possible, I would stay here myself!" He embraced and kissed me then sat down beside me. He was unable to speak any further because of the deep emotion he felt and the thought of such happiness he had experienced on that day, at that hour in being so close to a saint.

I must recall at this point that when we were children, we recited our night prayers at father's table, and we were attracted by a book that my mother would tell us not to touch because it was father's book. When I was older, I discovered that the book was St Francis de Sales' *Philothea*. A picture of the saintly Bishop of Geneva hung on the wall in the same room. Any time we misbehaved, mother used to send us to recite an 'Our Father', 'Hail Mary' and 'Glory be' before the picture. As a result, we looked upon St Francis as a saint who forgave and blotted out all the wrongdoing in the world. Our family had a devotion to this saint, on whose feast day, January 29, 1886, father died after having received the blessing of Don Bosco to whom he had offered all his children. What a marvel of Divine Providence which makes everything serve for the glory of God and our spiritual well-being!

My father visited Don Bosco in his room after attending a play performed in Latin. He told him about all his sons and daughters and was advised to send the girls to the Daughters of Mary Help of Christians at Mornese and the other boy, Stefano, to Alassio. He spent a few days at the Oratory before going to Alassio. Filled with satisfaction and joy, he acknowledged my Salesian vocation as a further blessing from heaven on the whole family. The subsequent close relationship between Don Bosco, Fr Rua and my family was a special, providential grace.

Meanwhile, I was still coughing blood and consumption followed. I was given Holy Viaticum. Mosca, the infirmarian, who was well known to the older Salesians, asked me to remember him in heaven. The doctor made very brief visits and prescribed turpentine pills to stop the bleeding. I lay resigned, awaiting my last hour.

One afternoon, I heard Don Bosco's familiar footsteps outside my door. He knocked, opened the door and came in. He wanted to know how I was and what I was eating. Seeing the remains of an egg on my plate, he asked if I would eat a bit of roast meat as well. I answered that I was fine, and I begged him to hear my confession. Then I told him, "I made my request to go to the missions in America, but I think they have already gone and come back." He gave me a significant look and making a sign to me with his outstretched hand, he said, "You will go, you will go! I will now give you the blessing of Mary Help of Christians." Taking off his *biretta* and joining his hands with a devotion that inspired confidence and trust in the power of God and the intercession of Our Lady, he gave me his customary blessing.

The blood ceased to flow at once, my cough disappeared, and I felt hungry. I was coming back to life! It was mid-February, the most unfavourable time of year for my illness as my room never got the sun, and yet I improved noticeably day by day.

Fr Rua, who came to see me often, paid me one of his welcome visits at the beginning of the month of St Joseph. When I had given him a lengthy account of the schools in which I had been educated, he assured me that I would be cured and told me that all I had observed and experienced during my three years with the Benedictines, the long years at the seminary and the time I had spent at the Oratory would serve me well in the Salesian houses in which I would work. He then encouraged me to spend the month of St Joseph well and told me about some graces obtained at the Oratory through the devotion to this great patriarch and our heavenly patron. I improved so much that on the feast of St Joseph, I was not only able to say Mass in the infirmary but could even listen to a sermon given by Fr Barberis in my place, since at the beginning of the year I had already been chosen to speak of my patron saint. I was also present at the ceremony that the good artisans gave in honour of their councillor for the professional school, Fr Giuseppe Lazzéro and all the Josephs at the Oratory.

Don Bosco paid me a second visit and hearing that his blessing had chased away my illness and had given me a good appetite, gave me a rule, "You can begin to eat a bit more, but see to it that you don't eat anything that disagrees with you." In Confession, when giving me my penance he would say, "Ask God for the precious gift of health so that you can later use it in His service."

We treasured the advice that Don Bosco gave us in Confession. I know that some of my companions kept a little notebook in which they immediately wrote the inspiring words spoken by Don Bosco both in the confessional and in his room. For us they were like the word of God that came from heaven for our good and to guide us through life. We often meditated on them during difficult or dangerous moments, drawing comfort and encouragement from them, imagining that we were close to Don Bosco whose presence and words encouraged us to follow him in his saving mission among young people.

Fr Rua continued to visit me often during the time of my convalescence, prudently offering me some light work such as drawing up the rough draft of the *Letture Cattoliche*, and he recommended that I take short walks. I loved the city of Turin, the Eucharistic City, from a religious point of view. I therefore planned to visit all the churches that took turns in having perpetual adoration.

As I was going to make one of these visits, a strange thing happened. I met Don Bosco in the playground surrounded by a group of boys, and I approached to kiss his hand. Seeing that I was carrying my hat, he asked, "Are you going out?"

"Yes, I replied, I am going to take a short walk as Fr Rua advised."

Don Bosco held on to my hand but continued to speak with the others. After a while he turned to me and repeated, "So you are going for a walk?"

"Don Bosco, if you think I should not go, I will gladly remain."

But he did not answer one way or another, nor did he let go of my hand. Then he said again, "Going for a walk, are you? Good, very good."

I stood there bewildered, thinking to myself that perhaps I shouldn't go. I couldn't fathom what Don Bosco meant. He let go of my hand at last saying, "Off you go for your walk."

I walked along the avenue towards the Church of the Crocetta where there was adoration of the Blessed Sacrament that day. But when I was some distance from the Oratory, I felt such severe pains in my heart and lungs that I was unable to breathe. Then I thought, "Don Bosco surely knew that something serious was going to happen to me." I no longer had the strength either to go ahead or to turn back. I leaned against a tree until the pains subsided and then very slowly made my way back to the Oratory.

After dinner, while walking with Don Bosco I said to him:

— *You asked me three times this morning why I was going for a walk. You must have known that something was going to happen to me.*

— *Oh, and what happened?*

— *I had a severe pain in my heart which I thought would kill me. I had to stop and rest before returning home. I thought to myself; Don Bosco warned me insistently. In short, I realised that I should not have gone out.*

— *I think you're a fatalist,* he replied looking at me with a smile.

Though I was convinced that Don Bosco's blessing had brought me back from death to life, during the time of my convalescence I had a hidden anxiety to recover my strength completely once and for all. Therefore, hearing about any tonic or medicine I was easily led to try it. Now it happened one evening after supper that I was accompanying our dear Father to his room, and he asked me how I was. I answered that I was convalescing well, but that as a precaution I was taking tonics so I would recover sooner and be able to resume my work. Don Bosco allowed me to go on talking and then with his usual fatherly smile, coupled however with a resolute tone, warned me, "Who lives on medicine lives in misery."

These words were the best cure in the world for me because they taught me to put aside all anxiety, to do away with exceptions and to return at once to the common life. He discovered the weaker side of his sons immediately by conversing with them, and therefore, with a word, or a sentence along with a smile and a joke he corrected and encouraged us urging us to be more generous and thus better prepared for our mission.

This was how all of Don Bosco's words, even those spoken in jest, centred our being, bound us closely to him and made us attentive and obedient even to his suggestions.

I'll give you a further example. While my body was recovering, my spirit also seemed to acquire new strength by which it rose to higher aspirations to be zealous and apostolic. Urged on by my imagination and with strong enthusiasm, I wrote a long letter to Don Bosco thanking him for having restored my health through the intercession of Mary Most Holy. I placed myself in his hands to dedicate myself to the education of boys of every social condition, to teaching catechism, to preaching to the people, to circulating the *Letture Cattoliche* and to look after the sick. I wanted to take up the last item mentioned because I had heard some of my fellow priests who had just come to the Oratory complaining that we had no ministry to the sick here as the Jesuits do, though in fact everything that charity could suggest was already being done for the sick.

I delivered my letter to Don Bosco naively thinking that he would call me and approve of my plans and thus open up a new field for my activity and revive aspirations. No way! When I next met Don Bosco, he passed me by. I kissed his hand and he spoke to me, smiled at me, but there was no word on the subject of my wild dreams. Finally, after a week had passed, I approached him and got up enough courage to ask if he had read my letter. Don Bosco looked at me and smilingly answered, "Yes, I read your nice letter. I thought it was a letter from the Holy Father. Everything can be answered by two words: our Rule. Everything is there." I was deeply satisfied with this response. It seemed to me that I could hear our Divine Redeemer saying to me as he said to Martha, "There is need of only one thing."

During that memorable year, Don Bosco continued to hold the attention of both Salesians and students with his Good Nights in which, from time to time, he recalled the famous dream of the six and two 'dear to his heart'. I remember how one evening he said, "Let us spend Carnival time in holy cheerfulness, but let us not forget about vigilance and prayer in order to avoid falling into temptation. One of you who are listening to me will not see the end of Carnival time." We wondered if it would be one of the six or one of the two. We soon found out, when a boy quietly passed on to a better life after just a few days' illness. During this time, he was well assisted by the Superiors and members of the Sodality to which he belonged. This was the first time that I had been present, though only in the choir since I was still convalescing, at a Requiem service and the tender ceremony of the burial of an Oratorian. The procession of the boys, the clergy singing psalms, the St Aloysius and Blessed Sacrament Sodality members who accompanied or carried their deceased friend, gave a sense of heartfelt piety. This was one of the acts of a genuine Christian and Salesian education.

Don Bosco, who never lost an opportunity to reawaken the holy fear of God in his sons, and who constantly repeated the "be vigilant" of the Gospel, came that evening to give us the Good Night. After speaking about the boy who had died, he recommended that each of us should offer other practices of piety in addition to the ordinary prayers of suffrage for his soul and continued, "While one of us did not finish Carnival, there is another who will not finish Lent nor spend Easter with us." At that time, I was already out of bed and saying Mass in the infirmary where they had installed a beautiful little altar. I celebrated there in the midst of the sick and those who were convalescing. We never lacked for patients since it was winter. We were already in Holy Week and there was no one who felt that they were so ill as to be the one indicated by Don Bosco. On the Tuesday of Holy Week that preceded the day on which the Oratory Boys were to make their Easter Duty, I was already at the end of my Mass when I became aware of a boy approaching the altar to receive Holy Communion. Since I had not been advised, I was obliged to regretfully tell him, "I have no consecrated hosts, but you can receive Communion tomorrow." The boy quietly returned to bed undoubtedly thinking that he would be able to approach the Sacred Table the next day. That very night, however, he was stricken with an attack that brought him to death's door. There was scarcely time to give him Extreme Unction and Absolution.

Once again Don Bosco's prophetic words had come true. That night he recalled the virtues of this member of the Blessed Sacrament Sodality and offered him as an example. Fortunately, the boy had been well-prepared. The result of this event was not only a genuine spiritual resurrection on that Easter, one that was fruitful in firm resolutions, but it was also a revelation to us that Don Bosco was a friend of God and that his words contained many warnings from heaven.

Chapter 11

The Pedagogy of the Oratory

At this time, I could say that my convalescence was over, and I was gradually getting back to my former duties with a few extra ones that put me in contact not only with the Salesians of the house, but also with outside works. My experience of the life I had embraced was thus increased. I was very fortunate with my change of room. I had the second one on the second floor overlooking the gallery where Don Bosco passed several times a day on his way to his room. I often accompanied him, especially in the evening, and I always took advantage of the opportunity to speak with him confidentially. Indeed, he himself was kind enough to inquire about my health, occupations and impressions and to explain some point of the Salesian plan of action to me.

My next-door neighbour, the councillor for schools, Fr Pietro Guidazio, was an excellent confrère and known by all to be a good-hearted man, entirely consecrated to the fulfilling of his duty in accordance with Don Bosco's method. He kept in close touch with teachers and assistants and also with the pupils, especially those of the higher classes. His room, therefore, was visited frequently, especially during the last two hours of evening study. Only a door and a thin partition separated us, so without sinning through curiosity or indiscretion, I could hear the disciplinary and scholastic consultations and the teaching problems that were solved there. In this way I received first-hand lessons that made me appreciate the school of Don Bosco and his method more and more, because usually the difficulties were resolved with a last, decisive word: Don Bosco says this, Don Bosco does that, Don Bosco likes things done in this way, that is the custom or tradition at the Oratory.

Let me give you an example. One evening, Fr Guidazio was visited by an assistant who was somewhat annoyed with a pupil because of lack of respect, stubbornness and arrogant replies in the presence of other boys. The assistant was very annoyed and thought that the disrespectful student should be given a lesson in public by being deprived of recreation for a day and his supper. The good councillor listened patiently to the story, deploring the incident and simply uttering a few sounds of amazement. Afterwards he made a few remarks on the fiery character of the boy and promised to call him for a serious rebuke since he well knew that bad example had been given. He was sure, he said, that the pupil would think about his attitude and make amends by behaving better in the future.

The first part of the punishment was dropped, substituted by a correction from the councillor and the promise of amendment from the boy. A few words were then exchanged about depriving the culprit of part of his supper and leaving him on bread and soup. Finally, Fr Guidazio exclaimed in Piedmontese: "*Par dui prüss* (for two pears, the usual portion at supper in those days) do you want to enrage a poor boy? You will see that we will use a more effective and salutary means. Leave it to me!"

Having dismissed the cleric and more or less convinced him that characters are not easily corrected by punishments, he called the culprit. This was the most interesting and instructive scene for me. Fr Guidazio inquired about the boy's health and studies. He then wanted to know if he had any problems and if he was happy at the Oratory, had he been to see Don Bosco and so on and so forth. Having discovered that he had no difficulties with his studies and was satisfied with Oratory life, he asked about the incident with the assistant and let him talk, although the boy, who was embarrassed and humiliated, did not take all the blame.

Then the tactful councillor made him see that he would have to correct his proud behaviour and be respectful when he received corrections. He suggested that the boy go to the assistant, ask his forgiveness and sincerely promise to make amends by his good example. He also added a good word about being prayerful and the opportunity for spiritual direction from Don Bosco that would put everything straight. I heard a few sobs. The boy was moved and did not even want to go to supper. When the time came, the same assistant invited him to go in and assured him that everything had been forgotten. From then on there was a complete change in the boy who was often seen walking with his assistant and mingling with other companions. It was very natural that the pupils who were treated so gently would cherish happy memories and sincere affection for those who had wisely guided them along the right path.

I learned other useful things in the prefect's office where I was during the holidays at the beginning of the new scholastic year. I was working there to enter the names of the new students and artisans into the registers. How benevolent the Oratory was in a reasonable, prudent and educational way! When the name and surname of the student or artisan had been recorded in the register, the following was added in ink, "Received for three months at the normal rate (then 25 lire a month) and after that according to merit." Therefore, during the first three months the students had a strong incentive to behave well. The parents, who in most cases made real sacrifices to pay the expenses, constantly urged their sons to study and behave properly. This was the reason why the boys look their conduct marks seriously, since a merely satisfactory mark, a *fere optime,* as it was then called, was received with tears at the weekly public reading by the prefect, especially knowing that immediately afterwards the grade register was taken to Don Bosco's room. He, in turn, studied his boys and applied the appropriate measures, giving them the help they needed through his Salesians.

The effects of Don Bosco's educational method were revealed to me also through another channel. The prefect sometimes gave me the letters that the boys received and sent out. I fully realised that this responsibility obliged me to be discrete and reserved. I must acknowledge that the piety and goodness in the parents and the simplicity and good will of the students were a great help to me spiritually. The boys usually talked about school life, enthusiastically describing feast days, walks and dramatic entertainments and gave news of their studies and conduct. Here the praises of the councillor for schools abounded. They told how he spurred them on with his encouraging words, spoke to them about people and events at home and asked them for news of their families. There would also be praises for other Salesians who had more direct dealings with the individual boys. Needless to say, when the parents replied they showed themselves to be deeply grateful for the attention to their sons, and expressed their gratitude to this or that Salesian, so that it seemed like a single, spiritual family was formed around the boys.

However, I also received a different kind of lesson in Salesian pedagogy. I would like to write of one in particular.

First of all, Fr Rua tested the candidates by having them conduct a Catechism class for either the boarders or oratorians. I was privileged to teach the former. I readily understood how reasonable it was to begin from where Don Bosco had begun. The class assigned to me was composed of two sections from the first preparatory class, and each section had sixty students. There were 120 boys crammed into a room that was large, but for so many restless boys! I prepared myself in seminary fashion, with a nice little introduction divided into three parts: the importance of the catechism, advantages of this study and the manner of applying oneself to it. After the prayer and a few introductory words, a low whisper began to run through my pupils (all new boys, few accustomed to school, and none to boarding school). The whisper soon rose to a disquieting crescendo, drowning out my feeble voice and making further progress impossible. One of the boys in the class looked at me with compassion and made a sign to his companions to keep quiet and to listen to me. All in vain. I stopped abruptly several times and there was a moment's silence. I even raised my voice and they looked at me in surprise. Then the noise began again and drowned out the explanation being given by the poor catechist who nervously awaited the end of the lesson. Finally, the bell rang. After the prayer I left the classroom a discouraged man, while I could read in the eyes and expressions of the boys a sense of pity for my sad situation.

I immediately went to Fr Rua and told him about the unhappy result of my first experience. He smiled at me as usual and tried to cheer me up:

— *Look, that happens to everyone the first time because the job is new, and you cannot take it all in at once. Next time it will be much better.*

— *Oh, Fr Rua, I have already taken in the experience and it has taken me in too! I have little hope of improving. There are too many boys, they are all new, my lungs are weak, and my character is anything but strong. I have no practical experience.*

— *My dear son, try again next Sunday. You will see that things will get better. We'll help you. Look for an interesting story to tell them and that will get their attention.*

The following Sunday I tried to practise what Fr Rua had suggested. I even had my story ready, but I could not get to the end of it. Although they seemed rather more open at first, those in the back, perhaps because they were unable to hear very well, soon began to talk and this overpowered my voice. The second defeat left me completely dispirited. I thought to myself, "I entered an educational institute and cannot even teach catechism as I did in my parish church and in the evening classes. How am I going to cope with the rest?" Fr Rua encouraged me with the assurance that such difficulties would disappear with practice and when the pupils were more disciplined. Sadly, in fact I was relieved of this duty.

However, my uneasiness, as you can imagine, did not cease. I therefore had recourse to Don Bosco and told him about the two unsuccessful attempts and the doubts I had about my ability to cope with the principal duties of a Salesian, i.e., teaching Catechism and conducting classes. He smiled and asked me how I could be so intimidated by a hundred or so boys who were well-disposed and anxious to listen and learn and that the difficulty lay in the fact that we did not know each other.

— *How can we get to know one another?*
— *Join them, treat them in a friendly way and be like one of them.*
— *Where and how am I to join them? I'm not made for playing, running and laughing in their company; my poor health, my chest weakness hinders me.*
— *All right, then. Go to the pump. When it is breakfast time you will find a crowd of boys waiting there to drink. They will be talking about studies, school, games and everything. Go among them, make friends with everyone and your success will be guaranteed.*

The suggestion gave me new life, although I did not then understand its importance. I was determined to do exactly what Don Bosco had advised. Breakfast time came and I look up my position beside the pump of the old well near the Pinardi House. The pump is still there today, but now it has drinking water obtained from above and no longer from under the ground.

In those days breakfast consisted of the famous *pagnotta* (bread roll) that was given to the boys as they came out of church. As they received their ration, they would run over to the pump, have their breakfast and then scatter to play their games. There, where they crowded around the pump, was the strategic point indicated to me by Don Bosco.

So there I was at my observation post, my Jacob's well, so to speak. I walked very slowly under the porticoes without losing sight of the pump or the boys who swarmed around it, *pagnotta* in hand. While some were drinking, others were chatting about lessons, homework, conduct marks and other school topics. One talked about the difficulty he was having in essay writing; another spoke of his aspirations without making any mystery of his vocation.

I approached, joined in the conversation, asked questions about school things of the day, enquired who the best in this was or that subject, and even brought myself to ask what they thought about catechism. I gradually saw myself being surrounded by a crowd of those rascals who had given me such a headache in class and who were now respectfully answering. I plucked up courage to ask them why there was all the noise during *my* lesson. There were many explanations from which I could see that we did not know each other and therefore could not understand each other. I returned to the same spot for several mornings and then boys came freely, showing that they had the best intentions.

While I was standing there chatting, for a few mornings I heard a bell being rung by a boy who went around the playground. At once several groups or boys ran over to the stairs that led to the rooms under the church. I asked what the bell was for. They answered, "It's for the St Aloysius Sociality meeting... for the Blessed Sacrament Sociality meeting... for the Altar Boys meeting... Then the members of those sodalities explained about their meetings, weekly practices and customs. In short, everything contributed towards giving me a more exact idea of the spontaneity that accompanied the education imparted by Don Bosco.

Often in the course of the years as I struggled against serious difficulties, I recalled the well "that Jacob gave to his son, Joseph (Jn 4:6) and told myself that we should never he dismayed and that in the long run there is a remedy for everything in this world!

At that central place in the Oratory, the site of the beginning of the work, one could see the spirit that animated that throng of boys. During the frugal breakfast and exciting games that followed, a cry and applause would suddenly break out, "Viva Don Bosco!" There would be a rush to greet him, to kiss his hand and to win a smile or a word from him. Making his way from the church to his room Don Bosco would be followed across the playground by a slow, joyful procession. He would pause often, talking to one or another about their appetite and health, always being their friend and by his fatherly glance spreading a wave of cheerfulness, good will and enthusiasm for doing good. The picture displayed on the great door of St Peter's in Rome on June 2, 1929, and later in the main centres of the old and new world, showing Don Bosco being carried in triumph by his rascals, is the pinnacle of his educational method: religion, charity, fatherliness.

This educational system did not only produce temporary effects, i.e., effects that were limited to the time the boys spent at the Oratory, but it also had an influence over them in later life. I realised this during one of the most beautiful and touching scenes at which I was present in 1877. It was the occasion of the celebration of Don Bosco's feast day, transferred that year from the day of St John to that of St Peter in honour the archbishop of Buenos Aires, as we will see later on: I want to allude to the Oratory Past Pupils' Convention.

Since 1870 the past pupils had been gathering on such occasions to pay homage to their Father with speeches, poems, songs and gifts of a kind that would please Don Bosco who preferred religious objects to adorn the altar of Mary Help of Christians. The promoter and organiser of that manifestation of affection and gratitude, the heart of that gathering of filial love was Gastini. It was June 29, 1877. During the great performance, in the midst of the speeches, singing and instrumental music, a long line of past pupils, preceded by their band, entered the hall. The surprise, joy and emotion of the spectators reached a climax. One of the group, who was a good speaker, explained the meaning of this event and the object of their gathering. It was the feast of their Father. The oldest and most indebted sons were returning from the world to their father's house to show their gratitude, to enjoy the delights of his fatherly embrace, to hear a good word and to rekindle their fidelity to the principles they had learned and the practice of the education they had received. The sight of grown men, for the most part labourers, but also clerks and professionals returning to the Oratory like young boys and rejoicing at seeing Don Bosco, moved the onlookers profoundly. This was a spontaneous demonstration of the gratitude of working-class people; it was also the evident fruit of Don Bosco's spiritual fatherhood.

It did not end there. An invitation was extended to return on the following Sunday to eat the bread of the Oratory and of Don Bosco following the custom that had been introduced by him which continues to this day, of having a special celebration for the past pupils. Therefore, during the early hours of the following Sunday, I witnessed the arrival of older boys and mature men, many already fathers, who had come to visit their Father, first in church where they went to Confession, served or assisted at Don Bosco's Mass and received Holy Communion. The rest of the day was spent in the purest joy and culminated in a fraternal banquet during which friendship and fidelity were renewed amid the most heartfelt expressions of affection. On the following Thursday, the same spiritual feast was repeated for the priest past pupils, among whom Don Bosco was truly at home. I was beside myself with admiration and astonishment.

Chapter 12

The Church of Mary Help of Christians

Fr Rua, who followed everything, allowed me to return gradually to my former duties and wanted me to get experience in everything. He re-entrusted me with the responsibility for the sacristy of Mary Help of Christians. People came to request graces and blessings from Our Lady. I had the duty of distributing medals among devotees, receiving their offerings and collecting accounts or the wonders worked by our heavenly Mother.

For me, that Church and sacristy were a first-hand learning experience and a wonderful sight. There, our saintly Founder constantly exercised his special mission of hearing the boys' confessions, directing them in the ways of God, fostering piety and all the Christian virtues, thus awakening in their young hearts the most sublime aspirations for the Salesian apostolate and the foreign missions. He would go from the confessional of the confrères and boys to that of the faithful who awaited and detained him for hours on end, especially on certain days, there, close to the altar of St Peter where he usually celebrated Holy Mass at that time. Oh, how often the same people who had unburdened themselves to him, received his advice and begged his prayers at the altar of the Help of Christians, confident and sure of Mary's help, would approach my table to wait for the Servant of God to give the blessing of Mary Help of Christians to them and a medal or picture. I was acting as minister, witness and still more, humble disciple since I handed Don Bosco the medals and gave the responses to the blessing. It seemed to me that virtue and Divine Grace or power emanated and were shown in the works of faith and devotion and in the person of the blessed apostle of the Help of Christians. I, who had seen him at my bedside a month before blessing and healing me in the name of Our Lady, now saw something supernatural shining in his countenance and radiating from his person. We prayed with him, shared his prayerfulness, fervour and confidence in asking graces and miracles from his dear Madonna who was already popularly called *Don Bosco's Madonna.*

Having lived for a year with our good Father at the church built by him in honour of the Help of Christians, how could we missionaries, scattered all over the world, fail to experience the urgent need of building churches and altars in her honour to draw young, rather, all Christians, around her? This is the explanation of the prophetic motto, *From here will go forth my glory.*

Domenico Palestrino already worked in that sacristy devoting himself entirely to the service of Our Lady's church. We got along and understood each other very well. He accompanied me when I visited the church for the first time since my illness. Having reached the sacristy, I asked if our dear Madonna had bestowed any extraordinary grace during my absence.

    — *Oh yes,* he answered simply. *She has granted amazing, beautiful graces.*
    — *Have you recorded them?* He took the register from the drawer and showed it to me saying: *This is one of the most beautiful graces. A stroke!*
    — *Good Lord, deliver us! This is one of the worst misfortunes.*

With wonderful simplicity, however, the good sacristan insisted that I read his account. The grace, in fact, was this: two girls, about to lose their mother who had had an apoplectic attack and had lost the use of her senses, made a triduum to Mary Most Holy asking that their mother might regain consciousness so that she could receive the sacraments or at least make an act of contrition and prepare for death.

On the third day, the patient opened her eyes as if waking from a deep sleep, showed that she was perfectly conscious, said the act of contrition with her daughters and then, kissing the crucifix. died! The girls had come to thank Our Lady, certain that their good mother was saved. The mistake, therefore, lay only in the catchy title which the sacristan had used for even greater effect.

I had to have a word, too, with Palestrino because of the disturbance which his excessive piety was causing the occupants of the room above the sacristy. When he had locked the Church, he used to go into the sanctuary to say the Rosary out loud. He seemed to be chanting it with singular enthusiasm, to our annoyance we may say, since we were unable to get to sleep. I asked him the reason for his behaviour and was told that he had adopted that method of saying the Rosary for some time to avoid falling asleep during the recitation. Really, he must have been very tired after his day's work. However, he would not neglect this tribute to Our Lady, feeling himself obliged, as her guardian and servant, to be her most fervent client. I was greatly edified by his reply and always considered Palestrino a precious gift and worthy model of the coadjutors sent to the Oratory by Mary Help of Christians. All of us missionaries on our return to Italy for the General Chapters were greatly helped by this confrère who generously supplied us with sacred vessels, church furnishings and helped us to procure all the objects for worship which we needed. He had acquired outstanding skill in these matters.

The holy month of Mary came. As Fr Rua saw that I was already stronger he suggested my sharing in the preaching of the weekly brief talks in the chapel of the Daughters of Mary Help of Christians. I chose the subjects inspired by the bouquet of flowers which Domenico Savio had given Don Bosco in his memorable dream: the **ear of wheat** at the centre (holy Communion), and around it the **lily** (purity), the **rose** (charity), the **sunflower** (obedience), the **violet** (humility), the **gentian** (mortification). This was my first practice in delivering sermons and I offered it to Our Blessed Lady through Don Bosco and Domenico Savio.

Either Don Bosco or Fr Rua gave us special counsels and timely practices every evening during the novena of Mary Help of Christians. They used everything as an opportunity to urge the boys to be devout to Mary Most Holy. In those days when the decoration of the church was still incomplete, the beautiful picture of the Help of Christians painted by Lorenzone hung in a prominent position but was rather unadorned. They thought, therefore, of improving the appearance of the sacred image which already inspired such devotion, giving it a special appeal. To this end the silver hearts which surrounded the picture itself were taken down from the wall. As Don Bosco spoke to the boys at the *Good Night,* he pretended to be amazed that the symbols of the piety and devotion of the faithful and the testimonies of so many wonderful graces obtained from Most Holy Virgin had all disappeared. He asked them for an explanation, and they replied, "They have been taken down to be polished and then replaced more resplendent than before around the altar of Jesus and Mary."

"And that," resumed Don Bosco, "is just what we have to do for Mary Help of Christians, namely, to polish our hearts; to renew and beautify them by means of a good Confession."

On the eve of the great feast a red velvet drape appeared around the picture with a large number of silver and gold hearts which stood out magnificently on this striking background. When the boys were paying their visits to the Blessed Sacrament and Our Lady during recreation, they stood spellbound at the sight. They had already learned from Don Bosco the meaning of what was going on, but he explained it again telling how they could give their hearts to Our Blessed Lady so that she could offer them to Jesus. This gift of their hearts was to be made permanent by entrusting them to Our Lady that they might always belong to Jesus. This could be done by frequent, devout Communions. It was truly a learning experience; one of those lessons which are never forgotten. In our case the lesson was repeated every time the boys raised their eyes to the picture of Don Bosco's Madonna.

I personally witnessed a wonderful incident which occurred on the eve of the feast. It was a prelude, so to speak, of the graces and miracles with which Our Lady rewarded the piety of her servant and his boys on the actual feast day. At approximately 9am a woman came to my "desk of graces". With her she had a sick girl of about twelve who could hardly walk. She wanted Don Bosco to bless her child who for many years had been paralysed and unable to speak. I pitied the good woman and still more the poor girl who, being unable to stand, was placed by her mother in the very chair which Don Bosco used when hearing confessions. When I learned that Don Bosco had begun his audiences, I called a few people to take the woman and the child to him because she would not have been able to climb the stairs with only the help of her mother. The latter had explained that the girl's right hand and side had remained paralysed after an illness, and she needed to be supported from that side.

Count Carlo Cays of Galetta and Castellette was already in Don Bosco's waiting room. He had come to ask the latter for a final word of advice about this plan to become a priest. When the woman came in with the girl, this good president of St Vincent de Paul Society who was so sensitive to the sufferings of others approached them, enquired about the little girl and with the consent of those present gave them his place. When the person who was with Don Bosco came out, he ushered them in.

The Count himself told me what happened immediately afterwards (and recorded the incident in the *Bollettino Salesiano*).

— *Do you have confidence in Our Lady?* Don Bosco asked the mother while she was still at the door.

— *Oh, if only you knew what it has cost me to bring my child this far! If it were not for my confidence in Our Lady and all her blessing, I would never have come.*

Don Bosco turned to the girl and said:

— *Make the sign of the Cross, then, and let's say a Hail Mary. No, not with your left hand child. Christians make the sign of the Cross with their right hand.*
— *She hasn't moved that hand since her paralysis,* explained her mother.
— *Oh, have courage and confidence in Mary Most Holy.*

Saying this, Don Bosco took the girl's hand, raised it to her forehead and told her to go ahead and make the sign of the Cross. The girl then made a perfect sign of the Cross unaided, pronouncing the usual formula with Don Bosco. Full of joy she turned to her mother and exclaimed. "Our Lady has cured me!" But Don Bosco who was overcome with emotion interrupted her, "Let us say a *Hail Mary*". The girl recited the prayer with ease amid the tears of her mother and the exclamations of the people who had crowded around the door. Mother and child then knelt down for Don Bosco's blessing, returned to the church to offer their thanks and went home rejoicing. A month later we saw the whole family coming back to fulfil a vow they had made.

My account would be incomplete were I to omit one particular circumstance. Count Cays had already decided, "If the miracle takes place, I shall consider it a clear sign that God wants me to become a priest and a Salesian". When the miracle did actually occur, he joined our Pious Society.

Since 1868, the year of the consecration of the church, the feast of Mary Help of Christians had always been kept most solemnly both by those living at the Salesian Oratory and by the countless devotees who came from far and near. Pilgrimages also came from distant places. We at home, the first to benefit from Our Lady's favours, experienced unusual fervour, a kind of joy and spiritual satisfaction which was quite inexpressible. We would have liked the ceremonies to have lasted the whole day. There were endless Masses and Communions. Great numbers of people approached the altar rails uninterruptedly from the early hours until midday. This is what the beautiful devotion to Mary Help of Christians does: it leads people to Jesus that he may redeem and save them.

On that great day of the miracles of Mary Help of Christians, we witnessed extraordinary, mysterious scenes. People, many obviously well-to-do, prayed fervently amid tears and sobs. They withdrew in the sacristies and choir: first absorbed in prayer, then at the feet of a confessor, finally at the altar rail. Though there were silver and gold hearts representing material graces around the picture of Mary Help of Christians there were still more human hearts raised to her on her feast days to praise, implore and thank her.

Chapter 13

Fr Paul Taroni

Under the spiritual direction of Fr Paul Taroni, the seminary at Faenza was for me, as for many other natives of Romagna, a true Salesian novitiate. Fr Taroni maintained constant contact with all of us in general and with each one in particular; thus, he knew us, advised us, and was always at our disposal. Both in confession and private talks he understood us perfectly. He possessed Don Bosco's spirit to a high degree and spread it wonderfully far and wide. As I have mentioned elsewhere, I wrote to this beloved Rector frequently from the Oratory. I spoke very enthusiastically in my letters about the feasts of Mary Help of Christians, which I eagerly looked forward to and in which he, too, desired to participate. I mentioned the matter to Don Bosco who told me to invite him to the Oratory in his name. In his biography of this Servant of God the famous historian Lanzonì has given an account of the devout pilgrimage he made. I shall keep strictly to this account, the details of which are quite exact.

Fr Taroni gladly accepted the invitation, all the more so since he had been longing to come in person to this church to offer his thanks ever since 1870 when he had obtained a cure through Mary Help of Christians, as he himself recorded ten years later.

Having reached the station at Porta Nuova on the evening of May 16, he hailed a cab to take him to Valdocco. While on the way he could not resist the temptation of asking the driver about Don Bosco and the Oratory to find out from some of the people what they thought about the priest he venerated and loved so much. The following dialogue ensued:

— *Who is this Don Bosco one hears so much about?*

— *A priest with a lot of schools. All the rich people give him money. He is a millionaire.*
— *What does Don Bosco do with all this money?*
— *Buys more schools.*
— *Who lives in these schools?*
— *Boys of course!*
— *Poor or rich? Who maintains them?*
— *Poor, and Don Bosco keeps them.*
— *So Don Bosco spends his millions very well. He is certainly a holy priest. And what about you, sir? Do you ever go to Mass in the church of Mary Help of Christians and to Confession to Don Bosco?*

At that moment, writes Fr Taroni, I reached the Oratory. The last rays of twilight illuminated the lofty cupola of the church and the bronze statue at its summit. The harmony of the six bells and the great church organ reached my cars. I went in to look at the Help of Christians encircled with brilliant lights. From her imposing picture she seemed like a heavenly vision.

As he left the church and went into the Oratory, more or less the same thing happened to him as had happened to my father when he arrived. He saw a priest getting down from a carriage and coming towards the gate. He greeted him respectfully and asked:
— *Are you going to the Oratory?*
— *Yes, and you? Do you know somebody there?*
— *I know a certain Vespignani. Do you know him as well?*
— *Yes, and we are going to see him right now.*

While the unknown priest invited Fr Taroni to go first, the latter invited him to do so since he knew the house. He entered followed by Fr Taroni who asked him where he came from.

Just as they set foot in the playground we came out of the sacristy after Benediction. When I saw Fr Taroni, I left the group of confrères I was with and hastened over to him, first kissing the hand of the "unknown priest" whom I greeted:
— *Good evening, Don Bosco!* and then, turning to my visitor I said, *How are you?*

He looked at me in amazement:

> — *Did you say Don Bosco?* He queried, *Where is Don Bosco?*
> — *He's there beside you. This is Don Bosco!*

At these words Fr Taroni fell to his knees with arms outstretched and then clasping them he exclaimed:

> — *Ah, Don Bosco! I didn't* recognise *you!*

Don Bosco helped him to his feet and embraced him. He then asked me who he was and when I had told him he said, "I understand, I understand; this is that great enemy of Don Bosco! Fr Vespignani, take him to his room and leave down his suitcase Because he needs to rest. This evening at supper put him in my place to *boscheggiare* [be Don Bosco]. We will make peace tomorrow." He then kindly left us.

While I was accompanying Fr Taroni upstairs, he never stopped repeating, "So that was Don Bosco! Now I understand why he has written so many books and done so many other things! Did you see how calmly and peacefully he speaks and walks? It is easy to see that he is a saint!"

In his notebook, Fr Taroni had written all the graces he wanted to ask from the Blessed Virgin, namely, the grace of a happy death for himself and his dear ones, courage when faced by danger, for himself and his sister who was a religious, as well as holiness and success in studies for all the seminarians and his nieces and nephews. He had also written down all the questions he wanted to ask Don Bosco: about his method of guiding boys and hearing Confessions, about his views on the spiritual life and about the inspiration he sometimes felt to become a Salesian.

During the ten days spent in Turin he made a careful study of everything relating to Don Bosco, his works and his untiring activity and took notes on what he did and said. On the May 18, he went to Confession to him for the first time in his room and when he returned, he was radiant and told me, "I have put myself into Don Bosco's hands so that he can do what he wants with me. However, he said decisively, 'For the present you should go back to your seminary and look after boys and ecclesiastical vocations. This is your vocation. You will be a Salesian cooperator, circulating good books and especially the *Letture Cattoliche*'." After this the good priest was wont to say jokingly, "Don Bosco didn't want me; but I am getting my revenge by sending him my boys."

"This morning," he wrote in his notebook, "Don Bosco told me that he would have no difficulty in raising his hat to the devil as long as he let him pass by to go and save a soul." Again, he wrote, "On the 23rd I was with him in his room until midnight. I told him about the graces which I intended to ask from Our Lady the next day, including fortitude and courage. He answered, 'Add: *May my heart burn with the love of Christ my God*'. I made it into a short prayer:

> *Help me, O Mother of God*
> *To live and die in divine love*

Before leaving his room, he gave me his blessing."

"On Friday morning, the 23rd, I again went to Confession to Don Bosco in the sacristy where he was still hearing Confessions at ten o' clock. I asked for his blessing for my seminarians, and he answered like a saint: 'Yes let us pray that they may all become holy and if it is God's will that some may become Salesians'."

On the train returning to Faenza, Fr Taroni overcome with emotion, composed a sonnet which ended as follows:

> *O Virgin, O Don Bosco, O Salesians!*
> *Happy you, happy the world with you*
> *If it invokes the Help of Christians.*

In the notebook containing the impressions of his trip he wrote the words of Oedipus almost as a title: *The friendship of a great person is a gift from the gods.*

That year, people from Romagna flocked to the Oratory. Whether correspondence with Fr Taroni influenced the clergy of Faenza or whether the good education given to the boys at Alassio contributed to the propaganda, the fact remained that clergy and lay people began to come to the Oratory and visit Don Bosco, with the aim of having him establish foundations in Romagna. Foremost among those visitors were Fr Pompeo Pietroncini and Fr Saviero Grilli. I should like to record a story, about my unforgettable friend Fr Grilli. That particular year he was in the Pio Seminary of Rome to which the heirs of Cardinal Patrizi, disposing of the deceased prelate's library, sent many books to be sold to the students. Among these books, Fr Grilli found the manuscript copy of the *Rules of the Pious Society of St Francis de Sales* which Don Bosco had given to the cardinal, Vicar of His Holiness. He bought it for a few cents and wrote to me saying that he liked it and congratulated me on the article which says, "Our master shall be St Thomas."

l referred the matter to Don Bosco telling him where his precious manuscript had ended up. "Greet your good friend in my name," he said, "and tell him I am very glad that the manuscript has fallen into good hands." This goes to prove the saying: 'Words fly away but what is written remains', and one never knows where it will end up.

Chapter 14

Count Cays

After the feast of Mary Help of Christians, Fr Rua gave me the task, of, I would not say of teaching Count Cays, but of going to hear his lesson every day. The text he gave us was Charmes' Compendium which seemed easier and more suitable as it contained dogma and moral theology in the one volume. I was already acquainted with our distinguished cooperator and friend as I had met him in the festive Oratory of St Francis de Sales. He had been there in his capacity as president of the St Vincent de Paul Society, whose members were then catechists at the Oratory and also protectors and patrons of the poorer Oratory boys and their families

Everyone knew how carefully and judiciously this former Member of Parliament and city official used his influence on behalf of the poorest boys who attended the Oratory. Moreover, he had a way of urging them to learn catechism and to become good, giving them little gifts at the right time and place; that is why they all wanted him as their catechist. It was providential and typical of the work of Don Bosco to have won the goodwill, cooperation and even the personal sacrifice of so many noblemen of Turin who readily put themselves at the disposal of the holy Founder of the festive oratories with a view to increase its prestige. They offered their help to what they saw as the last means of salvation for the preservation of faith and Christian morals of working-class boys, whether they were students or workers.

Count Cays also possessed a high level of religious knowledge. Having already freely devoted himself to a study of apologetics he had a more than average ecclesiastical learning, so much so that Don Bosco had him compile the annotated catalogue of the Sovereign Pontiffs which he was to include in his own Church History. He was fluent in writing Latin prose. That very year when offering a valuable crucifix which had belonged to Blessed Cafasso as a feast-day gift to Don Bosco, he added a beautiful dedication composed in Latin.

He applied himself, therefore, with such diligence to the study of theology that he always recited his lesson to me in Latin, though sometimes he would inadvertently lapse into French through force of habit. A sign, however, sufficed to bring him back to the language of the Church. He would ask for an explanation of everything making it obvious that he meditated on Sacred Scripture, and he was particularly knowledgeable on the Gospels and the Epistles of St Paul. In fact, he was already a master in these ecclesiastical subjects. Therefore, it is not surprising that when Fr Rua examined the Count on his theological studies, he told Don Bosco that he could become a priest as soon as he had made his vows. So he was ordained the following year, on September 20, 1878, to his own indescribable consolation and to the joy of Don Bosco and all his sons.

I should like to write several edifying pages about this Salesian priest who was for me and for all those at the Oratory a practical lesson of what veneration and love for Don Bosco could do in a person.

It was sufficient to visit Fr Cays in his attic room on the third floor and then to reflect on the comforts and worldly grandeur which he had forsaken, the case with which he had adapted himself to ordinary food, a humble room and strict community life to exclaim: this is another Francesco Borgia who sacrificed everything to gain the benefits of a heavenly home.

During winter when he suffered greatly from the cold because of his age, I found him in his little room wrapped in a green blanket taken from his bed but as cheerful and as witty as ever. He studied, prayed, and conversed with us in a friendly way without ever mentioning his family name or the things of the world. We heard him repeat, "I ask for three graces from Our Lady: first, to die close to Don Bosco and to be assisted by him; second, to be able to bless the members of my family that they may keep their ancestral faith; third, that I may not have to suffer a lot when I am dying since I have little patience."

He obtained all three. His death was so peaceful that he himself said to the bystanders, "I never thought it could be so sweet to die under the mantle of Mary and with Don Bosco at my side."

Chapter 15

Monsignor Aneiros

Immediately after the feast of Mary Help of Christians, solemn, providential events occurred one after the other showing that this indeed was the year of expansion towards the missions which had begun with the dream of Dominic Savio. The first of these events was the arrival of his Excellency Leone Federico Aneiros, Archbishop of Buenos Aires with a company of Argentinians including Monsignor Brid, Vicar General, and Fr Pietro Ceccarelli, parish priest of San Nicolas de los Arroyos. They were on their way to Rome to celebrate the Golden Jubilee of episcopate of the Holy Father, Pius IX.

Out of gratitude to such outstanding benefactors of his growing missions in America, Don Bosco went to Sampierdarena to meet them. The archbishop, who disembarked at Genoa, reached our school just as Don Bosco was concluding the celebration of Mass. Hearing that the rector, Fr Albera, wanted to tell Don Bosco at once of their arrival, the archbishop said, "Do not disturb a saint while he is recollected in his God after Mass." He waited for Don Bosco to come out of the sacristy.

Who could describe the meeting between these two great people? It truly seemed that those mutual acts of humility and affection, the warm embrace which they exchanged, marked the formation of a holy alliance between two apostles, representing all of Europe and America, to promote the redemption and salvation of many. They set off for Rome together to appear before the great Father of the faithful, Pius IX. In those two Patriarchs he would once again bless the entire work of Don Bosco and especially the missions in Argentina, on the joyful, solemn occasion of the 50th anniversary of his episcopate.

June 26 was a day of triumph and intimate union between His Excellency and Don Bosco. The pilgrims arrived at the Oratory via Milan and were presented by Don Bosco to his sons, pupils and cooperators. Church and Oratory were decorated for the occasion. From the entrance gate to the guestrooms Argentinean, Papal and Italian flags were in evidence. For the first time the band struck up the National Anthem of Argentina. Hearty cries of *evviva* accompanied the archbishop, Don Bosco and all the guests as far as the first gallery of the central building. From there Don Bosco introduced His Excellency with an expansive gesture and a strong, emotional voice, "Here is our Archbishop of Buenos Aires," he exclaimed, "our benefactor!"

For the next three days it was my good fortune, as sacristan, to assist at the Mass of this beloved archbishop with whom from that year to the end of his life (1894) I had a close filial friendship. Oh, with what great pleasure I recalled his visit to Blessed Don Bosco and the Oratory. For us missionary Salesians in Argentina he had the affection and fatherliness of Don Bosco himself.

During lunch on that day, a charming incident occurred, which greatly edified those at table. When it was time for the toast, the famous Gastini came along to sing and recite his verses in honour of Archbishop Aneiros and Don Bosco. The effect was so graceful and pleasant that one of the Argentinean priests, Canon Ciarcìa Zuniga, who was a cheerful and expansive character, having laughed heartily at the witty lines, called the author over and gave him a silver coin. Gastini thanked him, kissing his hand and then graciously placed the money in Don Bosco's hand. The canon, admiring this generous, spontaneous action summoned the minstrel again and said, "If I had wanted to give Don Bosco a present, I would have given it to him. I gave you that money for yourself. Now take this and keep it." But with the second coin in his hand, dear Gastini went ever more eagerly than before to Don Bosco and handed the money to him. Hearing the canon repeat, "It is yours; it is yours!" Gastini remarked, "We all belong to Don Bosco. Here there is nothing we call our own; everything is his." The Canon put an end to the matter by saying, "I won't give you the third coin." As he observed when later recalling the incident with lively pleasure, he would never have succeeded in making him keep even one for himself. Such was Don Bosco's first past pupil.

However, the greatest manifestation of affection and veneration took place on June 29 when a triple feast [was celebrated], that of St John, Pope St Leo II and St Peter. These were the patrons of Don Bosco, Archbishop Leone Federico and of Pietro Ceccarelli. The Oratory playground was transformed into a spacious theatre with various tiers of seats for the cooperators, the public and approximately a thousand boys. Opposite these a big canopy was set up with three armchairs beneath. The best one in the centre was for the archbishop and those on either side were for Don Bosco and Fr Ceccarelli respectively. When Don Bosco led His Excellency to his chair, however, there was a problem. Archbishop Aneiros wanted Don Bosco at all costs to occupy the place of honour. The edifying contest which followed provoked a burst of applause from the spectators. Finally, the humility of both prevailed for it was decided to leave the chair vacant in honour of the Holy Father, Pius IX as this was the feast of the Prince of the Apostles.

There was singing, music, recitations in Italian, Latin and other languages. There were scenes from home and great emphasis on the Argentinean missions of the Pampas and Patagonia. Gifts were offered to Don Bosco. It was, in short, a varied and most appealing entertainment. Archbishop Aneiros then rose to speak in that wonderfully spontaneous manner that had previously characterised him as a Member of Parliament in his own country. He praised Don Bosco and his work, exalted the beauty of Turin, the city of the Blessed Sacrament and of Cottolengo.

His Excellency went on to say that he had come to thank Don Bosco for his missions in Argentina but also to ask for many more Salesians. "My gifts to Don Bosco," he said, "on his and my feast day are my archdiocese and the whole of Patagonia. I offer souls to be saved, millions of souls. I offer every child in Argentina; I offer the indigenous people of the Pampas and Patagonia. I, too, have been to your little room, Reverend Father, and seen the scriptural motto which was that of St Francis de Sales before it was yours and which you chose for your Congregation: *da mihi animas, cetera tolle*. You ask for souls and I give you and your Salesians as many as you could wish for. Therefore, send us good missionaries; keep on sending your sons to Argentina every year. We shall always welcome them as your sons and our own, help them in their work and surround them with affection and great care. We shall always see in them the image of their great Father our most Reverend Father Giovanni Bosco."[3]

Having said this, they kissed each other's hand and ended up in embracing each other amid the unending, enthusiastic applause of all those spectators

---

3   Archbishop Aneiros never wanted to say *Don Bosco* because he said that for them *Don* was a title given to any man and that he did not understand the way we used *Don* for priests.

who were moved to tears at the sight. They had understood, more or less what the archbishop had been speak about. Nevertheless, Don Bosco requested Fr Ceccarelli to translate from Spanish and he did so at once with great ease and accuracy. He concluded to a further storm of applause.

Our Mother and Help of Christians, however, had a new surprise in store for that solemn moment as though she wished to seal the close bond of friendship between Don Bosco with his Oratory and Archbishop Aneiros with his mission lands of Patagonia. The young girl, Giuseppina Longhi, who had been miraculously cured a month before on the eve of the feast of Mary Help of Christians was present on the edge of the crowd with her mother and father. The family had come to testify and confirm the grace which I described in a preceding chapter. Fr Rua was anxious for this lively, talkative girl dressed in yellow to be introduced to His Excellency. She went up the steps of the platform with agility, kissed the archbishop's ring and Don Bosco's hand. She then told His Excellency all about the miracle with great simplicity while Fr Ceccarelli acted as interpreter. The archbishop blessed her and gave her a medal.

Privately, then, something wonderful happened. While the parents were signing the report of the miracle drafted by Count Cays, Don Bosco told the girl that she too should sign. Her father excused her saying that she did not know how to write. "What!" said Don Bosco, "such a big girl never went to school and never learned to write her name?" The truth was that she had been able to write before her paralysis but not since. Having heard this, Don Bosco insisted, "If she knew how to write before, she should also know now because the Madonna does not do things halfway." Placing the pen in her hand she signed her name at once with ease.

Fr Lemoyne, who had previously published a few booklets dealing with the exploration and conquest of several regions, particularly Mexico and Peru in the *Letture Cattoliche* series, had also written a moving drama about Patagonia entitled 'A Hope'. There could not have been a better opportunity for the presentation of this highly successful drama. It was well prepared and presented. Archbishop Aneiros admired it and expressed his wish that the wonderful events prophesied particularly in the last act might become a reality.

On June 30, the Archbishop of Buenos Aires and his company set out with Don Bosco for Alassio and spent a few days on that charming Riviera. They then proceeded, still accompanied by Don Bosco, to Marseilles from where they set sail about the middle of July. The pilgrims had counted on being in Buenos

Aires for the feast of the Assumption. However, Don Bosco in bidding them farewell and assuring them of the prayers of his young people warned them that they would not arrive as early as expected despite their own calculations and those of the captain. He added, however, that nothing serious would happen on the voyage. In fact, when the vessel was nearing the Canaries, the propeller broke, and they lost a week for the necessary repairs. Needless to say, the pilgrims did not reach their destination for the feast of the Assumption. We heard about this prophecy from several of those who were present.

On disembarking at Buenos Aires, the archbishop was pleasantly surprised to see the first school for artisans temporarily opened in the premises leased from the St Vincent de Paul Society. The band was composed not only of artisans but also of priests and clerics. It offered a new and very pleasant sight to the first cooperators who witnessed this typically Salesian welcome for their beloved bishop. As the latter expressed his thanks and appreciation, he declared that he imagined himself to be still in Turin with Don Bosco, whose blessing he had been asked to convey. Indeed, he was so edified while in Turin that he immediately published a magnificent pastoral letter in which he invited the clergy and people of his extensive archdiocese to support and help the work of Don Bosco.

The pious archbishop had also brought home a most valuable souvenir for his archdiocese and indirectly for all the dioceses of the Republic. He had admired how, throughout the year, the beautiful devotion of the Forty Hours was held in different churches in that city of the Blessed Sacrament. Now he decreed that all the churches and chapels of the capital should celebrate this devotion in the same way. He desired that these hours of adoration should coincide, if possible, with the titular feast of the church or chapel concerned so that the function might be more solemn and better attended. Our Salesian churches in Buenos Aires adopted the ritual used in the Motherhouse with sung vespers, sermon and Benediction every day. In the course of a visit to us several years later, Archbishop Aneiros assisted at this sacred function and said, "Now I understand why God blesses the work of Don Bosco so much and why He blesses every place in which the Salesians pitch their tents! It is because you treat Jesus in the Blessed Sacrament so well."

While the archbishop was on his way back to Argentina, the head of the first Salesian missionary expedition, Fr Cagliero, was being welcomed home by Don Bosco amid the cheers and wholehearted enthusiasm of the Oratory. He had come to give an account of the abundant harvest he had found in Argentina at the Italian church in the Genoese suburb of Boca and among the young people of Calle Tacuari in Buenos Aires. He also spoke of the prosperous future promised by the boarding school at San Nicolas de los Arroyos and, better still, gave the joyful news of the likelihood of being able to go to Patagonia in the near future and set up mission centres there. The enthusiasm engendered by the conferences, the Good Nights and the sermons of this great missionary surpassed all imagination. No one thought or spoke about anything else except the missions of America. The aspirations which resulted, though perhaps fantastic and poetical, did produce great good because they kept alive the missionary ideal in all hearts. Don Bosco, Fr Rua and Fr Barberis more than all others kept this missionary fire burning.

Chapter 16

A Missionary in the Third Expedition

Things had gradually reached a stage where Don Bosco could prepare a third expedition. He made no mystery about it with his sons, nor did he have any secrets, as he used to say, when speaking to his boys. Therefore, he asked them to pray that God might enlighten him in this most important undertaking. We surrounded our beloved Father to hear news and also to catch a word indicating to us who would be the lucky ones.

Who would have thought that Don Bosco would have chosen someone from the infirmary or from the convalescents' table, where they needed special attention? The fact remains that one evening in August he came into the refectory rather late, after all the others. I was sitting at the table with others who were in poor health. I remember how we looked at each other: those who had earaches, headaches or a slight fever, and consoled each other by laughing at our ailments. Suddenly, I felt someone pulling my hair from behind. I swung around to catch the practical joker and found Don Bosco who pointed at me and whispered, "Nothing stands in the way." I wanted to know what his words and gesture meant, but since Don Bosco was smiling, I thought it must be a joke. I gave it no further thought.

However, the next day the mystery was solved. After dinner Fr Rua called me and with his usual kindness said, "Won't you have a cup of coffee with Don Bosco?" There was no need to ask me twice. I went straight over and kissed Don Bosco's hand. He joked a little with me and those who surrounded him while the coffee was being poured. I, too, took my coffee after the others and was about to sip it. Meanwhile, Fr Rua took out one of those lists, which he always carried for giving notices, recommendations and such like, and asked,

"Don Bosco, do you want me to read the names of those who will take part in the new missionary expedition?" Don Bosco nodded. Then Fr Rua read Fr Giacomo Costamagna's name followed by my own and then those of others.

I was so taken by surprise that I could not hide my reaction. I blushed, then with a smile looked at Don Bosco and Fr Rua as though to say, "You planned this." In a flash Fr Rua gently asked me, "Were you astonished when you heard your name? Have you any difficulties?" I answered promptly in the negative and Don Bosco added, "You won't go until the doctor has given you a thorough examination and declares that this voyage cannot harm your health." In fact, when he asked the opinion of the doctor, the latter assured us that far from harming me, the sea voyage would do me good.

But what was the meaning of the mysterious words: "nothing stands in the way" which Don Bosco had spoken when preparing me for the great news? It was very simple. The saintly Founder went ahead rapidly and surely in his enterprises. Scarcely was the first house established in Argentina (a few rented rooms and not a foot of land) when he asked the Holy See if he might open his own novitiate in Buenos Aires. The decree dated July 6, 1876, duly arrived from the Sacred Congregation for Religious. Therefore, the hair-pulling and mysterious words repeated emphatically concerned this decree, or rather they marked the beginning of its implementation. In our saintly Father's smile, I seemed to discern a heartfelt joy and satisfaction and now I also saw his great hope for many vocations, especially among the sons of our good Italians and Spaniards, who would come from those lands. Don Bosco wrote to me at the beginning of 1881 (and addressed me in the familiar second person for the first time). "I Bless Our Lord who has given you sufficient health to work in this great need. God grant that you may be able to form a numerous band of candidates, novices, professed and finally very fervent Salesians!" Vocations were uppermost among his aspirations and formed the great dream of our saintly Father.

I had to undergo another little trial from my family. My elder brother came to visit me, partly for his own pleasure but also to meet Don Bosco. He went to Confession to Don Bosco and was greatly satisfied with everything. Without his suspecting it, he had the beginnings of a serious eye disease: purulent conjunctivitis. He suffered severe pain, both his eyes were closed, and he was afraid he would go blind. I served him in every way, but I did not know what else I could do to help him.

A homeopathic doctor had recently entered as a candidate and when he had examined my brother, he prescribed certain remedies to be taken with water. I had to go downstairs to draw some water from the pump which that doctor never found sufficiently clear and pure. He rejected it each time, so I had to keep going up and down the stairs. It would not have been so bad if the remedy had worked! But the patient got worse and one morning began to cry out, "I want Don Bosco to come and give me the blessing of Mary Help of Christians, otherwise I shall go blind." I tried to calm him by telling him that Don Bosco was in the sacristy surrounded by many confrères, artisans and students who were going to Confession, so it was impossible to speak to him just then. I would go later. He could not be convinced to wait. "Go quickly to Don Bosco, I know he will come at once."

I went and found the Servant of God besieged by penitents. I informed him of my brother's condition in a few words and he answered that he would come at once. The news that Don Bosco was coming to visit him pacified my brother somewhat. Oh, what charity! Don Bosco consoled him, blessed him and gave me a note of recommendation for Doctor Rignaud, the famous oculist. My brother was touched by Don Bosco's goodness which sufficed to calm him, though the disease was making rapid progress. When the specialist read the letter, he said to me, "I would go to the ends of the earth for Don Bosco. I shall be at the Oratory before noon." When Fr Rua was told that Doctor Rignaud was coming, he told me to inform the doorkeeper who was to let him know at once when the specialist arrived so that he himself could accompany him. "He is a very important man," Fr Rua said, "and must be treated with the courtesy and gratitude he deserves for taking the trouble to come here."

There was a bit of a misunderstanding. The doorkeeper was substituted by someone else at the appointed time and when the doctor duly arrived and asked for the patient with the eye trouble, he was told that there was no such patient in the infirmary. The specialist left his visiting card and went away. One anxious hour succeeded the other and only towards evening was the mistake discovered. What confusion for me and what displeasure for Fr Rua! The patient was getting worse and worse. Finally, he convinced me to go back to the doctor and explain what had happened. The doctor was kind enough to call for his carriage and return with me to the Oratory. He found that one of my brother's eyes seemed to be lost and he was in danger of losing the other. He was most understanding when I told him that my brother had a family but said he could only treat him in an ophthalmic hospital.

My brother, who was in a state of nervous tension exclaimed, "If I must go blind, I want it to be in Don Bosco's house!" We calmed him down, helped him to dress and go downstairs and the doctor kindly took him in his own carriage. I had to visit him every day at the hospital where infinite care was needed to bring about a complete cure. It was a great lesson to him who was so opposed to my entry into the Oratory. But for me it was such a shock that it had a serious effect on my already weak health. I developed a tertian fever[4] which affected me every third day with such vehemence that I was forced to stay in bed. At one moment my teeth chattered with cold, and then at another, the heat made me break into a heavy sweat that left me exhausted the next day. Fortunately, when the charitable Count Cays no longer saw me in his room he asked why. Upon learning of my sad condition, he brought me a very effective remedy, two tiny pills that a specialist in Paris had prescribed for his farm workers. These cured me of this serious illness so that we were able to resume our theology lessons.

It happened that a novice, Pietro Rota, was ill in the infirmary at the same time with the same fever that I had. I told the good Count, who hastened to visit the patient and cure him with the wonderful pills.

Despite this, (and this is why I mentioned the attack of fever), I must say that the unfortunate tertian fever recurred when I was in America and lasted much longer, even though it was milder. This started in 1880, the year of the Civil War in Buenos Aires with all the difficulties that followed. This time I was completely cured, not by human remedies but in the church of Our Lady of Lujan, as I celebrate the votive Mass of Mary Immaculate. This happened in 1883 when the novitiate began in Almagro. It was not in vain that Don Bosco, in the previously quoted letter, had expressed the hope of my being able to work. He was assisting me with his prayers. Meanwhile the names of the new missionaries were made public. The leader of the expedition was to be Fr Costamagna, a man of robust physique and tireless zeal. Such was his love for Don Bosco and the Congregation that he did not spare himself in his activity. He was an energetic preacher, an excellent musician and singer and a highly experienced Confessor and spiritual director. He was director at the house of Mornese, the cradle of the Institute of the Daughters of Mary Help of Christians. He single-handedly preached a mission to the people and spent

---

4   A type of malaria caused by the protozoan plasmodium vivax, it is the most common form of the disease, is rarely fatal but is the most difficult to cure and is characterised by fevers that typically occur every other day.

from morning till night preaching four or five times, giving special conferences and hearing Confessions. Understandably one had to be very quick to keep up with him. But at the same time, he had a great heart. As one who was at his side for fifteen consecutive years, I can assert that he accomplished unheard of things with apostolic and missionary zeal, forming a tradition of prayer, religious observance and pastoral life. At this school those who had a good spirit and a will to work got on well and learned much. His frankness, however, was not immediately pleasing to all, but afterwards they realised that he was right. In short, with that character of his placed at the service of the good cause, he created a magnificent mission.[5]

Our other companion, Fr Domenico Milanesio, at this time director of the Festive Oratory of St Francis de Sales, was destined to become the most persevering and heroic missionary of South America. He was always the humble and simple Padre Paisqno, (as he was known after becoming fluent in the indigenous language and adapting himself to the customs of the native Araucano-Tehuelche). Don Bosco himself had chosen him to direct his first Oratory, a model for those which later rose up everywhere, because of the zeal he showed in teaching catechesis, his constancy and patience in seeking out boys, even those of the streets encouraging them to attend the Oratory. He also had great zeal in promoting Gregorian chant, the St Aloysius and Altar Boy Sodalities and had wonderful ways and means of forming catechists and cooperators. Faithful to the traditions, customs and method of Don Bosco, he was convinced that by following in the footsteps of the Founder, with simplicity and perseverance, all abandoned young people could be saved.

This is how one began to be a Salesian missionary: by taking an active and constant part in all the activities of the oratories. This is the principal mission of our days because all the means of redemption are wonderfully integrated in it. There we find the Word of God, i.e., catechesis and the Holy Gospel, prayer taught and practised in common, and devout reception of the Sacraments. Consequently, young people are converted from sin to a life of grace and the holy fear of God is implanted in all. Here is the kingdom of God and His justice which the missionary will later spread to the world. Such was the work which Fr Milanesio engaged in for thirty-five years in Patagonia.

---

5   A biography of Fr Costamagna was published. It was written in Spanish by Fr Roberto Tavella and translated into Italian by Prof. Giovanni Gallo, *Vita del Missionario salesiano Mons. Giacomo Costamagna*, (Turin: International Publishing Company, 1929).

There was also another priest, Fr Tommaso Bettinetti, who had recently entered the Oratory. He was a former member of the Sons of Our Lady of Monza. Having had to leave that Community for health reasons, he had asked Don Bosco to give him a trial at the Oratory, hoping that Mary Help of Christians would cure him. In fact, after a novena suggested to him by Don Bosco, he was restored to perfect health. He immediately decided to become a missionary. He went to Argentina where he taught art and exercised the sacred ministry at Buenos Aires and San Nicolas and later at Montevideo. However, he felt that he could not completely adapt to Salesian life and accordingly obtained leave to become a diocesan priest. He died as parish priest of Bragado in the province of Buenos Aires where he was mourned by the faithful and greatly esteemed by the episcopal curia.

I must make particular mention of Fr Giovanni Paseri who carried out his mission at Colon, Montevideo and at Buenos Aires in the Pius IX College in which he was ordained priest, and later ended his days. He was the first rector of the school of St Catherine, Virgin and Martyr. His zeal attracted universal admiration, while his apostolic fervour in writing and hearing confessions led him to the sacrifice of his young life. An extensive biography has been written about him.

Two more of our dear companions, the clerics, Giuseppe Gamba and Pietro Rota, who are still living, would go on to represent and direct very important missions: the former in Uruguay and Paraguay, the latter in Brazil with its immense territories. How wonderful are the ways of the Lord! The members of the third expedition left the Oratory and opened the way for future Salesians into many parts of South America, moving successively from Argentina to Chile and Bolivia; from Uruguay to Paraguay and then to Brazil from which the missions spread to Matto Grosso, the Amazon and the Rio Negro. Thus, those first two foundations of La Plata formed a base for the foundations in Ecuador, Colombia and the surrounding republics. Is this not the story of the grain of mustard seed which grew into a gigantic tree? Do we not see here the morsel of leaven which caused a great mass to rise?

God also made use of the help given by other clerics and coadjutors as well as some non-Salesians who, because of their love for Don Bosco and a certain enthusiasm, desired to add their contribution to his missions. Among the coadjutors I would like to mention the master cobbler, Bernardo Musso of Castelnuovo who for forty-five years made great sacrifices to run the main workshop for that trade in the Salesian professional schools in Argentina with very good results. It was he who with that patience, charity and love of work learned at the Oratory, had the honour of teaching his trade to the first indigenous person of the Central Pampas, Vicente Diaz, raised in Pius IX College at Buenos Aires. Archbishop Aneiros had brought him home from Carrue after a mission which he preached there. He was the son of a chief called Manuel the Great, and showed good aptitude for work and study, so much so that he became a master cobbler in the school of arts and crafts at Viedma, Patagonia.

A former official and member of the Royal Guards also took part in our expedition. His name was Benvenuto Graziano. We saw him enter the Oratory in his resplendent uniform. He was a slim, good-looking fellow with fair hair and moustache, had a fine voice, outstanding talent for mathematics and the direction of workshops. He possessed a vast amount of technical knowledge, was exact and methodical in all kinds of artistic work. In short, he was a model director. Perhaps his designs and enterprises were too grandiose and hasty making them more commercial rather than educational, according to the method of Don Bosco. Yet he gave great service in establishing and organising workshops for the first Salesian school of arts and crafts in Argentina and the whole of America.

The way in which he decided to take part in our third expedition is worthy of mention. One day when walking along the streets of Rome where he was in military service, he met Don Bosco. He introduced himself at once to his former superior (he was a past Oratorian), kissed his hand and greeted him with great respect and obvious joy. Don Bosco asked him:

— *My dear Benvenuto, are you still Don Bosco's friend?*
— *Imagine! I have never forgotten my benefactor and never will.*
— *You know that friends cannot live far from each other but must always be near. Yet you are so far from me! Come to see me.*

Don Bosco then bade him an affectionate goodbye. The next day Graziano went to see Don Bosco and said:

— *What you told me yesterday about friends staying close and never parting made a deep impression on me. I couldn't sleep last night. I have come to say that if you will have me, I am   ready to come with you and then go wherever you send me provided I have the good fortune of being with Don Bosco and doing what he wishes.*

— *Well done, my dear Benvenuto; come to the Oratory when you can and want to. There will always be a place for you at Don Bosco's table. Afterwards we shall come to an agreement. Do come in your handsome military uniform; it will give pleasure to everyone to see a brave soldier of God in our ranks.*

Graziano was true to his word. A few days later, having first obtained leave and then resigned from the army, he came to Valdocco. We saw him enter the refectory with Don Bosco, behaving with the simplicity and affection of a boy. He later asked permission to go to the missions and therefore to prepare himself with us by studying Spanish. He did so with much enthusiasm and with such good results that he was soon teaching others. Certainly, it is easy to understand that in this missionary work he was lacking a foundation, and therefore a supernatural strength, so he could neither be perfect nor constant. Particularly in the early days, when there was great need and a shortage of suitable and well-disposed personnel, Don Bosco took people who were less ready, having at least made sure that the leaders of the expeditions left nothing to be desired.

I cannot fail to mention the cleric, Bartolomeo Panaro, who later became a priest and one of the most self-sacrificing missionaries in Patagonia. He was a companion of Fr Milanesio for many years in Chos Mala and then for twenty years rector of that house which is situated at the foot of the Andes in the territory of Neuquén. He subsequently shared his apostolate with another intrepid missionary, Fr Gavotta. Both have already received the reward promised to the faithful servant and good labourer in the vineyard of the Lord. To end this review of our missionary companions, I shall mention the cleric Galbussera who was particularly prominent in San Nicolas for his knowledge of pedagogy which made him famous even beyond the Salesian school. In fact, he was asked to form part of the Urban Scholastic Council. Nor was he less distinguished for his charity and diligence. Although rector of that high school, he had extraordinary intellectual and moral success in teaching prisoners. This charity occasioned touching acts of gratitude on the part of those unfortunates who, on being set free, would come to see and thank him. We know that some became real apostles of the Easter Duty with their relatives.

Here is an example for aspiring missionaries so that they may reflect on how to prepare themselves for the apostolate. All of us, future missionaries, priests, clerics and coadjutors, were assembled in the boarding school at Lanzo. It was recreation time and two of our younger companions were playing a game of skittles, I think. Then for some reason or another they became annoyed and offensive to each other. Our brave, former soldier Graziano intervened and twisting his moustache said, "Are you two really missionaries? How do you dare wear the uniform and bear the name of missionaries of Don Bosco? What you need first of all is a bit of military service to discipline yourselves and learn to conquer this coarse behaviour which scandalises us. I fear you are among those cowards who, to escape work or service to their country, flee to America."

All hastened over to hear this military harangue. Then Fr Mianesio approached me and said, "Let's go to Fr Cagliero and suggest that these two be excluded from among the missionaries." We did in fact go to Fr Cagliero and related what had happened although we admitted that the chief blame fell on only one of the two contestants. The good superior put his hand to his head and said, "What can we do? We would like to choose the best and send them to the missions; but good people are needed everywhere. Let us resign ourselves and pray." We left Fr Cagliero's room satisfied, and the two fiery young men did come with us.

But here is something to complete the lesson for the aforementioned candidates. Scarcely a year after our arrival in America, one of the two who had provoked the dispute at Lanzo, because of his difficult character, had already been moved from one to the other of the three schools whose rectors he had exhausted. He was greedy and had a weakness for fresh eggs. The school cook, who was a simple, pious and good worker and was deeply concerned for the good of the house, noticed that the eggs were always missing from the poultry yard. From his room he had heard a peculiar noise coming from the hen house and this had made him think that there were thieves. His suspicion was increased by the knowledge that there were prisons close by and that when the inmates were released, not yet having work, they lived on what they stole. Therefore, he hid, revolver in hand, ready to shoot after giving the usual warnings.

Later that night there was a flutter of wings followed by a general cackling among the hens. Our good Silvestro (as the cook was called) shouted out, "Who goes there?" The only answer was a louder commotion among the hens. He shouted again and, noticing a shadow moving, fired in its direction though the bullet was not released. The intruder calmly said, "Hey, there, what are you doing?"

— *Oh, farinel!* [rascal!], exclaimed Silvestro. *What kind of tricks are you playing on me and what a risk you have taken! Look at this revolver. A miracle has saved your life to teach you not to do such a thing anymore. Now let us put this weapon under lock and key in the infirmary. Go to Confession and Communion tomorrow and then we shall go down to the kitchen-garden to see if this gun will fire. This will be a sign that you are alive by a miracle.*

In fact, when they had both performed their devotions, they went along to try the revolver and found that it was actually loaded and when fired, a bullet was released at once. It seemed that the unfortunate fellow had learned his lesson. However, not long afterwards he left the missions to work elsewhere, where he fell victim to his hapless character which had not improved at the school of Don Bosco. With the exception of this one case, however, the Salesian spirit fostered by the Servant of God in his sons produced truly wonderful fruits in the other seventeen or eighteen members of the third expedition. May it be God's will to raise up new bands of apostles every year, such as we have seen to our admiration for half a century, to bear His Holy Name and the light of the Gospel to every region on Earth!

Chapter 17

Spiritual Preparation

The choice was made and those chosen had already formed a group or school under the general direction of Fr Cagliero and the immediate guidance of Fr Barberis. Fr Costamagna was devoting himself particularly to preparing the first expedition of the Daughters of Mary Help of Christians.

The final period of preparation consisted in a retreat. Towards the middle of August, we assembled with other confrères in the school chapel of St Philip Neri at Lanzo where Blessed Don Bosco began and directed the retreat which was preached by Fr Lemoyne and Fr Bonetti.

I still remember the beautiful Gospel pictures which Fr Lemoyne painted for us in his meditations, describing the Palestinian environment very well. He made good use of biblical studies and the information regarding the Holy Land which he had drawn directly from the sources. His easy, poetic and dramatic style kept us absorbed in the contemplation of the life of Jesus and allowed us to savour the beauty of His divine teaching. Indeed, Fr Lemoyne was a man of simple, ardent faith and all those who listened to him were enthralled. His sermons, then, gave us a very real idea of what Our Lord did, taught and suffered for the redemption of the world. Nothing could have been better for Salesian missionaries about to set out for a mission of evangelisation.

Following the meditations and interwoven with them were the brilliant, animated and interesting instructions or conferences given by Fr Bonetti on Salesian life. He painted a very fine portrait of the historical events of the Congregation with the important characteristics of the Salesian spirit as revealed by our Rule. All these talks were illustrated with sayings and deeds of the saints, but more so with the teaching and example of Don Bosco. Fr Bonetti's distinctive characteristic was his ardour and zeal for the glory of God and the salvation of souls, and his religious asceticism derived from devotion to the Sacred Heart of Jesus and to the spirit of St Francis de Sales. The missionary zeal of his heart overflowed in his words which were most appropriate for us who were preparing to extend the Kingdom of God in the world with the means pointed out to us by the nature of our Institute.

One of our group who admired such beautiful conferences was determined to make use of recreation time to ask Fr Bonetti for clarifications and norms on how to preach the Word of God with the same popular style and energy, with the same effectiveness which so pleased and captivated us in him. We strolled two-by-two through the little pathways in the garden. My companion and I followed closely behind Fr Bonetti and heard a real treatise on missionary preaching which that dear Salesian was explaining to our confrère. He told him how to make his introduction and win the attention of listeners from the outset; how to divide his sermon into points and how to develop them with increasing interest, adapting himself to his audience; and finally, how to tackle the practical part of the sermon and win over the will to make an efficacious decision to give oneself to God, thus changing [the person] and assuring one's salvation. I was supremely edified and understood very well why Don Bosco had initially intended Fr Bonetti to be the leader of the first missionaries and why he had suffered so much when insurmountable difficulties prevented his departure. Fortunately, God consoled him with the generous offer made by Fr Cagliero to substitute for Fr Bonetti! They were kindred spirits where the apostolate was concerned and two chosen sons of our blessed Father.

Don Bosco who presided over our retreat was nearly always with us for recreation. We surrounded him with the tenderest affection, clinging to his every word, listening to his counsels and recommendations, asking many questions, consulting him as to what could befall us in the future. We were determined to imprint the whole of his moral features upon ourselves and to drink all of his spirit from its source. It never entered our minds that we would not see or hear him again since, for us, Don Bosco was never to die. It was just that before leaving his side we felt the need to gather as many souvenirs and counsels as possible.

We made another general Confession to Don Bosco, receiving private advice, most consoling words and reassuring promises for our future work. It seemed that in those days Don Bosco drew on all the special gifts, let us call them, of his spiritual direction to strengthen us and give us a good supply of what we might need in the long, difficult and very distant mission which he was entrusting to us.

Allow me to make a digression. I learned from our unforgettable Fr Albera, of happy memory, that when preparations were being made for the First General Chapter to be held at Lanzo after our retreat, the Jesuit Fr Secondo Franco told him that the primary responsibility of the Salesians, the first task of those assembled there should be to form a religious conscience in all the confrères. We ourselves saw that in our saintly Founder's dealings with us he was aiming precisely at this lofty goal of forming an entirely Salesian criteria, conscience, character and spirit in each one of us. He made his teaching practical by imprinting his lessons on us with the fire of his charity and encouraging us to apostolic zeal by his wonderful example. What beautiful days we spent at Lanzo! It seemed as if we were on the Mount of the Beatitudes listening to the Divine Master as he expounded his doctrine and taught his apostles and disciples how to lead people to salvation.

Chapter 18

Two Dreams of Don Bosco

In those days Don Bosco had two prophetic dreams which seemed to refer to the missions.

The first dream concerned a new work which the Blessed Virgin was clearly entrusting to him, namely, the agricultural schools which would not only complete the professional school for working-class boys, but which would also produce fine clerical and priestly vocations to guide a vast number of poor young people. Impressed by this dream, Don Bosco immediately accepted the agricultural school of Navarre in France, that was offered to him a short time later and, as we read in the life of Don Bosco, events proved he had not been mistaken. However, several circumstances from his dream, which were not encountered there, led him to think that it not only referred to a particular French foundation but was indicative of a new work to be developed elsewhere, chiefly in the missions in America.

While on the subject I would like to speak about the origin of the first agricultural school in America. It arose from a suggestion or, if you like, a hint given by the Vicar of Christ, Leo XIII, in 1893 to missionaries in Uruguay and Argentina. During July of that year, Luigi Lasagna arrived at Buenos Aires as a newly ordained bishop. Great festivities were held at Pius IX College at Almagro where guests, friends and cooperators had assembled. When the tables were cleared the bishop told his listeners that immediately after his consecration, he had an audience with the Holy Father who asked him:

— *What special work have you Salesians promoted in America?*
— *Your Holiness, we have primary and secondary schools with boarders, day-pupils, festive oratories and professional schools.*

— Oh, not enough. You must found and organise agricultural schools in those boundless Argentinian plains. Those who go to America engage chiefly in agricultural and pastoral occupations. You should educate the boys in these occupations so that they may be better able to help their parents and through the practice of Christian life form sound moral and religious colonies.

Among the guests was a certain Mr Michele Nemesio Uribelarrea who had founded a colony to which he gave his own name and built a church, school and railway station there. On hearing what Leo XIII suggested he said, "I had 300 hectares of land in my colony which could be used, but I have given them to the St Vincent de Paul Society on condition that they build an agricultural school." By a providential coincidence one of the presidents of the same society was present, the lawyer Alessio de Nevares. He immediately stated, "We would not know how to establish an agricultural school in that territory and would be very glad to hand it over to the Salesians." The work began without further ado.

The first practical agricultural school was started in 1894 at the cost of great effort and enormous expanse. Today, there are ten of these schools in Argentina: three in Patagonia (Viedma, Fortin Mercedes and Choele Choel) and seven in the other two provinces of Buenos Aires and Cordoba (Rodeo del Medio, Vignaud, General Pirán, the above mentioned Uribelarrea, Carlos Casares, Trinidad and Pindapoy).

May the Lord send us the necessary personnel to make them better and better and more suited to the aim for which Our Blessed Lady inspired Don Bosco to found them.

Don Bosco narrated his second dream as a souvenir of that unforgettable retreat. In this dream he seemed to be walking by night along the narrow paths which lead to Valdocco. He was coming back from visiting a sick person. When he reached the crossroad, he saw a Lady at the side of the path turning the handle of a beautiful cylinder, like a mill for roasting chestnuts or coffee. He was amazed to see a woman at such a work at that time and place and stood watching her. The Lady looked gently at him and beckoned to him to come nearer, saying, "I am working for you and your people."

Seized with curiosity to find out what exactly he was seeing he approached, fixing his eyes on the Lady and the tool in her hand. She said to him lovingly, "Do you see? I am making sweets for your Salesians. Look at them." Don Bosco went closer and looked at the cylinder which was as transparent as crystal and was divided into three compartments. In each of these he saw different kinds of large sweets, pastilles or lozenges.

— *Take a good look*, said the Lady, *and you will understand everything. The sweets in the first compartment, as you see, are white, almost transparent and covered with dew which makes them shine in the sun. They are the sweets of perspiration for your Salesians who will have to toil and sweat in their work for the glory of God and the good of others.*

Don Bosco rejoiced at such a good invention because by making use of it his sons would be sustained and would acquire new strength in their apostolic labours.

— *Good, good!* said Don Bosco. *Let's have a look at the other compartments.*

— *These sweets here, as you see, are black. They are as transparent and brilliant as the others, but they are stronger and more powerful because they impart resistance and sacrifice even to death and any suffering for the same glory of God and for the benefit of others. Do you like them?*

— *Oh, yes!* answered Don Bosco. *God grant that we may all be strong until death as Our Lord teaches us in His Passion and Death on the Cross! Is that all we have to do for the apostolate or the mission of the Salesians for the salvation of young people?*

— *No, there is yet another kind of sweet. These are red all equally brilliant and dew-covered. They signify the martyrdom which your Salesians will suffer in their apostolic activity in different ways. This is the gift which I am preparing for them. It is your duty to explain to them where, how and why these sweets are made and distributed to those who want them.*

Having said that, the Lady disappeared and with her the strange cylinder. The preparation of the sweets was finished. Don Bosco realised that one had to be prepared to receive these beautiful gifts from Our Lady Help of Christians although the lesson was a hard one.

As he continued on his way to the Oratory, he saw Fr Picco coming towards him. What little hair he had was standing on end and he held his arms out as he shouted, "Don Bosco, Don Bosco! Defections at the Oratory! Persecutions against the Oratory!" At that cry and agitation of Fr Picco and other priests and confrères, Don Bosco said, "Never mind. Keep going forward in the midst of difficulties, disillusionments and contradictions. We have the sweets from the Madonna. They are different in colour and flavour; they provide the strength and stamina needed to resist all trials and conquer all adversity. We must take everything from the hand of Our Blessed Lady. She sees everything, arranges everything and converts everything into merit and a crown."

Upon awakening Don Bosco decided to narrate his dream for the instruction and comfort of his sons, so that the memory of it might sustain them and give them that peace of mind which confidence in Mary imparts to her devotees.

We who heard the dream were also witnesses of the defections and persecutions which befell the Oratory in those days, and we understood that the first one to taste the sweets of the Madonna had been Don Bosco himself. Hence, we were encouraged to acquire that confidence in Mary which softened the multiple trials of our missionary life. And how many of our dear and virtuous missionaries really tasted those sweets of perspiration, of sacrifice even to death and martyrdom, if not of blood, certainly of heart and mind!

However, they always did so with joy and serenity, always with determination and confidence in the protection of Mary who converted their hardships into victories and triumphs tor the good of thousands and millions of people who were saved for all eternity! These were the gentle hopes which crowned our retreat in 1877.

Chapter 19

Don Bosco and My Father

At every opportunity Blessed Don Bosco offered us wise and providential lessons for our missionary formation. It seemed that he wanted to give us an abundance of favours and signs of paternal affection. The feast of the Holy Rosary was approaching. It had been a tradition to celebrate this feast at Becchi where Don Bosco was born. There was a little room there transformed into a chapel and dedicated to the Most Holy Rosary. Since the feast fell during holiday and harvest time, Don Bosco took the opportunity to offer an enjoyable outing to the priests, clerics and those boys who had chosen to stay with him and give up their holiday at home. At the same time, he provided a novena of sermons for the local people with a solemn feast enlivened by the Oratory musicians. That year the future missionaries led the excursion.

Fr Milanesio went to Becchi the day before the novena and preached every evening. He was accompanied by many Sons of Mary or candidates to the novitiate who ran up and down the hills in all directions ringing a bell to invite the neighbours to the religious service.

The main group was to be in Becchi on the evening of the vigil. A band of musicians was formed, equipped with all kinds of instruments and a selection of songs. We went as far as Chieri by train and from there proceeded on foot, stopping in a field for a rest while the musicians played and sang, Graziano played the guitar, others the violin and a few the clarinet so that a magnificent concert kept the whole company cheerful.

At Chieri we visited the seminary where Don Bosco had studied philosophy and Theology with his dear friend Luigi Comollo who, after an early death, appeared to him one night in the dormitory. All present heard his voice. We also went to the Tana house to see the chapel which commemorates how St Aloysius gave himself the discipline to prevent his family from organising a dance which he feared might offend God. The adjoining house which had probably formed part of the same property at one time had been left to Don Bosco. I saw old parchments there belonging to the family of St Aloysius and a few family crests carved in the windows. We also venerated the cincture of St Thomas which is preserved in the church of the Dominican Fathers in the same town. We finally reached Becchi and waited there for Don Bosco who had promised to join us since he had been prevented from accompanying us.

The feast of the Most Holy Rosary was celebrated very devoutly. The pilgrimage fortified our spirit and increased our confidence in the power and goodness of Our Lady who had taken Don Bosco from this poor, remote hamlet to make him the Father of many young people and the founder of a work with a great future. That outing also offered us missionaries the opportunity of getting to know one another better and becoming more united in holy friendship.

On our way back we went through Mondonio and visited the cemetery to see Dominic Savio's grave. We also went to the house in which he had lived and prayed and in the room where he died. I remember the beautiful impression produced in me by Dominic's grave and home. It reminded me of my First Communion and the providential events which had led me to Don Bosco. A new era in my life was beginning, one consecrated to young people, to the formation of candidates, novices and Salesians. During this mission I asked Dominic Savio to help me to inspire his spirituality in all our pupils and future confrères.

A welcome surprise was waiting for me in Turin: my father's last visit. He had gone to see my two sisters in Mornese and there had learned from Fr Costamagna that I was to take part in the forthcoming missionary expedition to America. Such was my father's veneration for Don Bosco since his first meeting with him, that he dared not raise the slightest difficulty. When I presented myself, he greeted me affectionately and said, "So you want to sample the ocean water! Right, then I hope you will pay us a visit before you go. Mother is anxiously waiting for you."

"You know," I replied, "that mother is extremely nervous and that emotional upsets are very bad for her. Let us, then, spare her that suffering."

Father said nothing. He had lunch with Don Bosco and was so touched by the kindness and affection lavished on him that before leaving the table he took off a large gold chain that he was wearing and put it into his host's hand saying, "Take this little homage to Mary Help of Christians." Don Bosco blessed him with deep emotion.

As I was seeing him to the station at Porta Nuova, he spontaneously said to me, "All right, we shall also make the sacrifice of not seeing you at home. Don't worry about coming to say goodbye to mother. Just remember us every day at Holy Mass." This was the final farewell of that deeply Christian father whom I was never again to see on this earth. It was October 15, Feast of St Teresa. On my way back from the station, I went into the church of this dear saint to whom my father had given a sister and his eldest daughter, both Carmelite nuns at Ravenna. Both had made the same sacrifice with fervour and spiritual satisfaction. Even when one is experiencing natural emotion, the grace of God can bring contentment.

The First General Chapter presided over by Don Bosco ended during those days at Lanzo. All the General Council and rectors had been present at it. Fathers Secondo Franco and Giuseppe Rostagno of the Society of Jesus assisted a few times at the preparatory sessions held at the Oratory by Don Bosco with Fr Rua and the chapter members. I recall how on many evenings Fr Rua asked me to accompany Fr Rostagno to his residence near the church of the Holy Martyrs and how this priest spoke to me praising Don Bosco and his work. I was highly edified.

Chapter 20

Last Experiences at Valdocco

After having fulfilled many varied duties at the Oratory, I was given yet another responsibility which I fulfilled more or less successfully. I was to take the place of the prefect of this large house. The prefect, Fr Giuseppe Bologna, had gone to make his retreat in the boarding school at Lanzo and had asked me to take his place. "Ask for nothing, refuse nothing," I said to myself with St Francis de Sales; and somewhat fearfully I look over the responsibility.

Scarcely had I opened the office door on the first day, which was a Monday when a good woman appeared, fell to her knees and weeping told her tale of woe in the Piedmontese dialect. Amid sighs and sobs she constantly repeated: *Mi povra fumna* (Oh, what a poor woman I am!). I understood that her husband had given her the money to pay the rent and that she had lost it. She feared she would be beaten unless I gave her what was necessary out of charity. I urged her to search again saying perhaps she would find the money since it was impossible for me to give her the sum then and there. There was no way of getting rid of her. I promised to consult my superiors and told her to come back later.

No sooner was I freed from the first predicament then a gentleman appeared speaking French: a language which unfortunately was very little taught in my native Romagna. I concluded that he was a teacher and wanted to come and teach French at the Oratory. Since he knew practically no Italian, I tried to make him understand that we didn't need any French teachers. It was hard to get rid of him!

At last, when we were both tired of repeating the same thing, he left.

Immediately afterwards, a very smart looking Colonel appeared. Apparently, he had two sons at Lanzo and had come to complain that, in his estimation, personal cleanliness there was deficient or neglected. I tried to explain to him that the boys in our school were taught to keep themselves and their belongings in good order and that one could not expect to find as many servants as one would have in a family. Furthermore, I knew that the rector, Fr Scappini, had been obliged by order of the Holy Father, Pius IX to go to Rome to assist certain priests, the Concettini Fathers. It was inevitable, therefore, that direction at Lanzo should be disorganised. I racked my brain to settle the matter diplomatically, but it was not easy! The Colonel guessed that I had nothing to do with that particular school and that I was handling the matter without first-hand knowledge or responsibility. However, he was satisfied with my promises that things would be remedied the following year.

This was how the first day of my 'new life' passed. It was a kind of comedy with the most varied scenes and endless dialogue. During the days which followed there were further events which made me think about a rule given me by Fr Bologna, namely, to keep calm and gentle, to cut things short, to use few words, to listen, provide, give advice and then move on to the next job. Fr Rua was a model in this. He satisfied everyone, never changed, and never wasted a minute. I, too, seemed to be gradually succeeding in this responsibility which was also part of the Salesian mission and therefore had to be experienced.

Meanwhile I was being buried, so to speak, in correspondence addressed to the prefect. I packed it up and sent it to him with the following address: Rev Fr Giuseppe Bologna, Prefect in Retreat (!), Lanzo, Turin. According to the Rules, all correspondence goes to the rector of the house during the retreat and is not distributed to retreatants unless there is an urgent need, but I did not know that. The parcel arrived in the hands of Fr Rua who thinking perhaps that I was giving myself too much importance in my temporary responsibility, crossed out Fr Bologna's address on the parcel in which he put more Oratory correspondence and readdressed it to me in this form: Rev Fr Giuseppe Vespignani, acting vice-sub-prefect in the Oratory of St Francis de Sales, Turin. Now you see how Fr Rua's lessons work frequent, prompt, perfect and aptly given. They did me a lot of good!

In the course of these weeks God taught me a very useful though frightening lesson of a different kind. It was the defection of one of the aspiring missionaries who was supposed to be one of the key persons of our expedition. It seems that Blessed Don Bosco had foreseen this in the dream of the sweets. You will remember the cry of Fr Picco.

A priest had come to the Oratory from Bologna, a certain D.C., to become, as he said, a missionary of Don Bosco. He practised Spanish and made considerable progress in it. He spoke easily, preached fervently, and offered help in everything, so that he had dealings with all, and even claimed to be Fr Rua's secretary. He was seen serving Don Bosco's Mass at St Peter's altar. He often invited me to join him in saying the breviary to which he would add a little Chaplet of the Sacred Heart and other prayers. He seemed quite moved in the pulpit and made people weep. He addressed me using the familiar second person, but for my part I did not feel a spontaneous or serene confidence in him. A certain lack of prudence especially in prying into the affairs of the superiors did not go down well with me. During my convalescence he invited me to the station to mail some letters. On the way he stopped to join the funeral procession of a high-ranking official. I left him and he later re-joined me. It was then that he told me of his unusual missionary vocation. It is a lesson that could also benefit others.

It seems that when he had completed his studies and began to work as a curate in a country parish, he wanted to arrange a programme on the patronal feast with a band, fireworks and other amusements. The parish priest, however, intervened and changed things. This so displeased the curate that he handed in his resignation and decided to go to Milan to become a missionary with Monsignor Comboni. While on the train he heard someone talking about Don Bosco and his missions. He therefore changed his mind about going to Milan and went to the Oratory instead, seeking to be admitted as an aspiring missionary with heaven knows what dispositions.

He himself told me that after he had heard Don Bosco narrating the dream of Dominic Savio, he had gone to ask him to find out what he thought of the state of his conscience. The good Father, thus invited, disclosed many secret deeds of the priest's past life. Now it happened that while the First General Chapter was being held at Lanzo and our departure was drawing near, revelations were made which obliged this priest to leave us immediately. I was still in the prefecture in Fr Bologna's place when I saw D.C. arriving all hot and bothered to ask for the railway timetable and money for his journey. He then bade me a sad and mysterious goodbye and disappeared. When I asked Fr Bologna if he had left for good, I was told, "Yes, his missionary career has ended."

I was very upset, almost as disconcerted as I suppose the Apostles were at the Last Supper, when they heard about the terrible defection of one of their number. True, there had been symptoms; but the suddenness of what happened covered with the veil of mystery, just when there was so much talk of the approaching expedition, filled me with fear. I had to give Benediction that evening and as I knelt at the foot of the altar, my knees began to tremble, and I feared I would faint. Not even prayer could help me shake off that sad impression.

May God be praised! Now after more than fifty years we bow before the same altar and image of Mary Help of Christians to admire, bless and thank the Madonna of Don Bosco because her faithful servant succeeded in choosing, preparing and assisting the personnel of numerous expeditions so that his great work might extend, take root and prosper in many lands. The miracles of Valdocco were renewed all over the world. Replicas of the Church of Mary Help of Christians were built for the salvation of countless people. New generations of Salesians succeed one another in ever greater numbers. Indigenous missionaries rise up and legions of boys are cared for by the Congregation. Dismay, anxiety and contradictions of any kind fail to lessen or halt the work of Don Bosco which is the fruit of confidence in his Help of Christians and manifest proof of her maternal protection.

Chapter 21

From Turin to Rome

November 6 was the memorable date of our goodbye to the Motherhouse and to our saintly Father, Don Bosco. It was an unforgettable day because of the sentiments experienced: joy and sorrow, firm resolutions and uncertainly about the future, sincere gladness, but heaviness of heart due to the painful separation. Yet everything was dominated by unshakable faith in God, confidence in Mary Help of Christians and the reassuring words of Don Bosco who said, "Go in the name of God; I shall accompany you everywhere with my blessing and prayers. Do not fear; you will find everything in your favour. Remember the revelations through which we have been promised help for the success of our enterprises for the glory of God and benefit of all."

He stayed with us the whole day. We spoke to him in his room individually and collectively. Our confidence was increased by the presence and words of Fr Cagliero who had returned from Argentina after preparing a place there for each of us. He told us of the vast field of work and then described the present and future houses awaiting each one of us beyond the Ocean. The descriptions given by this great missionary, as well as his ardent enthusiasm like one returning from the exploration of that promised land, filled our minds with fervent hopes. They made us think that the historic hour of a great expansion of our Congregation had dawned. We were the fortunate champions who were to be the first to enter that future kingdom of God where miracles of redemption and grace would be worked. Indeed, our ranks included Fr Costamagna who on May 24, 1879, was the first to plant the cross in the heart of the desert near Choele Choel, on the banks of the Rio Negro and to celebrate the Divine Sacrifice there.

On the morning of November 6, community Mass was celebrated by Fr Costamagna and there was a general Communion of the confrères, missionary Sisters and all the boys. The Church was decorated, there were many members of the clergy, and much uplifting music. Everything helped to raise our hearts and bring down abundant blessings from heaven.

There followed a banquet at which we were bidden Godspeed by Salesians, cooperators and friends. This was followed by the evening service which I have previously described. What a time this was! Everyone felt close to God. As we distanced ourselves from all that is worldly, passions and material goods, we participated in all the divine gifts and our hearts were overflowing with heavenly consolations. As we had assisted at this same heartfelt, eloquent farewell the year before, the aspiration, vocation, resolution to become missionaries was born in us. We had reached our goal. The same noble desires were now resounding in the hearts of many; the same voice of Jesus was echoing in the hearts of many young men. This is the seed of missionary vocations passed on from year to year at this ceremony, which is so touching, so sublime and so full of divine teaching. It does one good to see generous young people overflowing with faith and love, leaving the people and things that they love, to go to faraway places in obedience to the call of God renewing the apostolate in the world.

Now Fr Cagliero went to the pulpit. He narrated the things he had seen in those distant lands as he travelled across three immense regions: Argentina with Patagonia and Tierra del Fuego, Uruguay and Brazil. He painted a very vivid picture of the neglected state of the Italians living there, concluding with these words, "Our first mission is to save our dear emigrants to prevent them from being lost." He was deeply moved as he outlined the plight of so many abandoned children in those immense cities who had no shelter, no Catholic school which could teach them some skill or trade. He told them about the foundation of the first professional school. He spoke of the prodigious zeal of the first missionaries who were asking for help so that they might not succumb like Fr Baccino who had sacrificed his life working among the Italians of *Mater Misericordiae*. He mentioned the excellent results of the two, lower and upper secondary schools, at San Nicolas, Argentina and Villa Colon (Uruguay) which were supported by kind cooperators of both those generous countries. He concluded by asking everyone for the support of their prayers and financial contributions for the work of the missions which is most important, meritorious and necessary since it perpetually renews the work of Redemption.

Crucifixes were then blessed and distributed by Don Bosco who whispered a good word to each recipient. There followed Benediction of the Blessed Sacrament, the recital of the *Itinerium,* the paternal embrace and the exit from the Church amid the tears, prayers and good wishes of those who had attended that magnificent ceremony. Don Bosco was the first to give this embrace. Fr Rua repeated it, followed by Fr Albera and it is now continued by Fr Rinaldi. Apostles succeed apostles, mission after mission is founded and people are saved by millions! *Adveniat regnum tuum!* [Thy Kingdom come!]

We set out for Rome under the leadership of Fr Cagliero. We were filled with great faith and devotion. We hoped to see Don Bosco again at Genoa before embarking. Several eminent ecclesiastics and cooperators were waiting for us in the Eternal City. They took us to *Trinità dei Pellegrini,* the historic hospice already sanctified by many outstanding personages who made pilgrimages to the tombs of the apostles. We visited basilicas, catacombs and monuments until the longed-for and blessed day of the Papal audience arrived.

Our hearts were flooded with joy at the thought of seeing the Pontiff of the Immaculate Conception, the great benefactor of Don Bosco and his Congregation and of receiving one of his last blessings since his health was already failing. We were led to a room in which other pilgrims of various countries were assembled. The Holy Father was brought in on the *sedia gestatoria.* As he was about to bless us, the angelic Pius IX said with a kindly smile, "Here are the Sons of Don Bosco."

"And here," added Fr Cagliero quite informally, "are the Daughters of Mary Help of Christians who are going to fulfil their mission in Argentina and Uruguay."

Having crossed the hall, the bearers set down the *sedia gestatoria* beside the throne, though His Holiness did not come down. His legs were badly swollen and ulcerated and he was unable to stand for long. He indicated that he was going to speak and proceeded as follows:

> In today's Mass for the Anniversary for the Consecration of the Lateran Basilica which is the *Mater omnium ecclesiarum* [Mother of all Churches], the holy Church applies these words to herself: *Terribilis est locus iste* [how terrible is this place]. Now, the Church is a most tender mother towards all her children, seeks nothing but the salvation of all peoples, scatters the seed of the Word of God everywhere, and sends messengers of peace to the most remote people. How then could so good and loving a Mother be called 'terrible'? Oh, my dear children! Yes, the Church is also terrible. [Here he raised his hands and made an energetic gesture

accompanied by a loud exclamation letting his red mantle fall back, and with a deep and penetrating look continued]: Yes, she is 'terrible' against her enemies, the enemies of those she wishes to save. You see what efforts are made nowadays to lead many young people astray. The seed of error is sown, a thousand means of corruption are invented so that people are lost, and society is perverted.

You missionaries and Sisters, Daughters of Mary Help of Christians, therefore, go out and look for many young people, protect them, bring them back to the Church. Do not fear the enemies of the Church; have compassion on them and try to win them back to the fold they have deserted that they may not incur divine punishment. My dear children, show your love for the Church, the Mother of all peoples, by defending her honour, and making her loved by all races and in a special manner by the young people among whom you will go.

So that your courage in doing good may never fail, I impart my heartfelt blessing. I bless all the pious objects which you carry with you. I bless your Superior in a particular way. I bless you, your relatives and all your undertakings. May this blessing help to sanctify you and all whom you are going to evangelise.

We then knelt down to receive the Papal Blessing. We were deeply moved and looked at the paternal countenance of this holy Pontiff as though we were in ecstasy, not knowing what to say. Such was the extent of our affection and veneration.

The Pope was carried around to give everyone a chance of approaching him and kiss his sacred ring and to allow him to address a few words to all. We kissed his right hand one by one with great feeling and received a private blessing. Some became quite emotional, repeatedly kissing his hand and presenting objects to be touched and blessed by him. A Portuguese lady who was next to me took his hand and pressed a huge Rosary against it. "Be careful, madam," said His Holiness, "you are hurting my hand."

While I was kissing the sacred ring, Fr Cagliero said to the Holy Father, "This young priest does not yet have faculties for hearing Confession. I ask Your Holiness to grant him the power of exercising the sacred ministry until we reach Buenos Aires." The Holy Father, Pius IX then said to me, "Hear Confessions, hear Confessions. I am now giving you all the necessary faculties. When you reach Buenos Aires go to the archbishop and he will grant you the permanent canonical faculties." I thanked the Holy Father, astonished that no one had ever spoken to me about such faculties. But because of my illness and the special circumstances of those years, faculties had not been asked for from the Curia at Turin. In this, too, I was really fortunate to have been granted the right to exercise so great a ministry so easily from the Holy Father.

We left the audience, blessing God and full of ineffable sentiments. We felt as though we were descending from Mount Tabor having seen Our Lord and spoken to him intimately like Moses and Elijah.

From there, we went to visit Cardinal Bilio, our distinguished protector and a great friend of Don Bosco. His Eminence received us in a very cordial manner and chatted with us about the Spanish language, the missions in America and the emigrants we would find there. He spoke of his particular affection for the Salesian work and his desire to entrust his seminary to the Salesians. We then went for a few moments to kneel at the tomb of St Peter to whom we prayed asking him to bless us and the missions confided to us by Don Bosco and the Vicar of Christ. The Divine Master had mandated the Prince of the Apostles 'confirm your brothers'. We wanted that confirmation from him, and we left completely satisfied with a great desire to work for the glory of God and the good of others.

The aim of our holy pilgrimage had been achieved. The blessing of Pius IX had been given for the third time to those pioneer Missions of Buenos Aires and Montevideo where the first and principal houses of Almagro and Colon were to be dedicated to the immortal Pontiff as a mark of everlasting gratitude. From these places missionaries were to go to every country in America. Oh, how truly rich in both earthly and heavenly fruits was that final blessing of the great Pontiff, Father of the Church and of our Pious Society!

A little incident initiated us into the anxieties and trials which alternate with great consolations in the lives of missionaries. At Trinità dei Pellegrini there was only one meal a day at about 10am, but we were not used to going to bed without supper. It is true that Fr Cagliero, an experienced missionary, and Fr Costamagna came to give us the *Good Night* in our dormitory and asked us if we needed anything; but we just looked at one another and thought it better not to make requests which might appear to be indiscreet. We did not know Roman customs and so we kept quiet. As soon as our two guides were gone, however we consulted together as to whether it would be lawful to scrape together a few cents from the bottom of our pockets and buy a bit of bread and meat. From 10 o'clock in the morning till 10 the following day seemed to be a dangerously long time to us. So we agreed that we could ask the manager to fetch us bread and salami which we happily ate. Things went alright for the first and second evening. However, on the return journey which took place on the third or fourth day, I, more than the others, suffered stomach problems that I was afraid that I would not reach Genoa. Thinking it was due to travelling by train, my heart sank at the thought of future journeys. Who would have believed, instead, that we would spend seven long days and nights in a train in Italy, France, Spain and Portugal without the least disturbance? It was that blessed supper which had spoiled everything.

Chapter 22

Last Days with Don Bosco

We met Don Bosco at Genoa. As soon as we reached him at the school in Sampierdarena, we surrounded him affectionately and gave him full details of the memorable audience we had had with the Holy Father, his words to all in general and to each in particular and our impressions of Rome. Don Bosco rejoiced and added beautiful reflections to imprint those memories more deeply upon us. One of our group the cleric Carlo Pane, had been obliged to remain in Rome because of a high fever. He belonged to my group and I had his name on the list in my passport. Don Bosco made enquiries about Pane, but it was impossible for him to re-join us, so our good Father could only recommend to us not to lose anyone else on the way. The cleric left later on with another expedition.

Meanwhile, I was seriously concerned about the difficult ministry of Confession asked for on my behalf, and obtained without my knowledge, but in agreement with Don Bosco following my regular course in moral theology, I had assisted at the twice-weekly conferences which the theologian Ascanio Savio gave to young priests at the Oratory. I had also received valuable advice and excellent explanations from our Father himself. Nevertheless, I felt the need of speaking to him about a point of the sacred ministry which would surely be a missionary's daily bread.

I happened to meet our dear Father in the choir of the church of St Gaetano, so I went to Confession to him. When I had finished, I told him about my perplexities regarding the duty of directing people of every kind, especially in the missions, where I would doubtlessly come across very difficult cases. Don Bosco listened with that great calmness of his and seemed to give due importance to my difficulties, but then he simply applied this text to me. "'Seek ye first the kingdom of God and his justice and all these things shall be added unto you.' Oh yes," he said, "let us try to establish the Kingdom of God's justice, guiding people along the path of grace, this is, in the practice of all the Christian virtues and along the path of prayer. These are the two important points; the rest will be added: special cases to be solved, advice to be given according to each person's state in life."

I still had two points to ask him, the chief one being hearing the boys' confessions and knowing how to help them deal with their bad habits. He suggested that I insist on the frequent reception of the Sacraments and the remembrance of the eternal maxims to help them practise the Gospel admonition "watch and pray", and that I should animate and encourage them always with devotion to the Sacred Heart of Jesus and to Mary Help of Christians. My other point concerned adults who had received the Sacrament of Matrimony. Here he told me to remember what the Roman Catechism piously teaches in these three points: 'faith is good, children are good, the sacrament is good', and to insistently recommend a good Christian life. These final lessons of Don Bosco were providential for me because in the Italian church at Buenos Aires I was assigned the care of our compatriots whom I often had to guide in the difficult moment of preparing for holy Matrimony.

Present at that time in Sampierdarena was commander Gazzolo, the Argentinean Consul whom God used to put Don Bosco in touch with the ecclesiastical authorities in Buenos Aires and San Nicolas. I had occasion to approach him. He already knew my destination and spoke to me about *Mater Misericordiae*, known as the Italian Church. He described its position at the centre or, as he said, "the heart" of Buenos Aires and praised the confraternity reformed by Fr Cagliero and flourishing at that moment. This made me think about and almost live my mission.

November 13 arrived; the day appointed for the departure of the main group of our expedition under the leadership of the ardent Fr Costamagna. Don Bosco asked me to accompany him in the little boat which took him on board the French steamer *Savoie* anchored in deep water at some distance from the pier. As we were rowed out to the steamer, a strong gust of wind blew Don Bosco's hat into the sea and while it was being rescued and dried, a good cooperator placed his own top-hat on Don Bosco's head who let him do it and thanked him. Then with wonderful serenity and gentleness, he looked at me sitting opposite him, and said, "You are thinking about your mother. But now I shall think about her." I answered at once, "No, Don Bosco, I am not too worried about her. When it is a question of God's will, she soon becomes resigned."

We had reached the steamer, and Don Bosco was once again wearing his own hat. He was met by all his sons who accompanied him to the lounge of the *Savoie* where they crowded around to enjoy his last words and receive valuable counsels. This was the third time Don Bosco had boarded this vessel to be with his sons whom he was sending to the missions. Each one heard a word of encouragement, a joke or a motto which sank deeply into his heart. He repeated the memento already given to the first missionaries and enclosed everything within the programme for his missions: to seek souls and not money, to be charitable and respectful with everyone, to take care of poor and neglected children, to have confidence in Mary Help of Christians and to enkindle all hearts with love for Jesus in the Blessed Sacrament by promoting religious instruction and frequent reception of the Sacraments.

He left his sons when the signal for departure was given. There was a touching scene which moved the onlookers to tears. All kissed his hand, asked for his blessing and recommended themselves to his prayers in words which were interrupted by sobs. Don Bosco was then rescued by Fr Cagliero and Fr Albera, the rector at Sampierdarena, and taken back in the little boat to the pier while his sons waved their hats and white handkerchiefs until they were out of sight.

Our little group remained behind under the guidance of Mons Ceccarelli, who was returning to Argentina. A short time previously, from Turin, Don Bosco had obtained the title Papal Chamberlain for him as a reward for his apostolic zeal and generosity towards our mission. Born at Modena he had received his degree in theology and Canon Law in Rome. When Archbishop Escalada of Buenos Aires died there during Vatican Council I, he had offered to accompany the remains to Buenos Aires. As a reward for his good services, the Buenos Aires Curia gave him the parish of San Nicolas de los Arroyos, one of the most important in the whole province. We were to have embarked on an English Royal Mail boat which was going to Lisbon; we were to procced by land to Marseilles and here board the vessel to head for the capital of Portugal. There was not enough time for this, so we were obliged to go by rail the whole way from Marseilles to Lisbon.

It sems that the reason why we had been separated from our companions was to be able to use the return ticket which the Government of Uruguay had given to Fr Cagliero. It fell to my happy lot to represent our first missionary and take his place.

A second touching scene, which I shall not delay to describe, took place at San Pier d' Arena. Don Bosco showed every mark of gratitude to his dear Monsignor Ceccarelli. Fr Albera did everything possible for us. His only regret was not being able to buy us an altar stone for the celebration of Holy Mass. We had a Missal, however, and read and meditated every morning on the Mass of the day and made a Spiritual Communion.

Our journey over land began on November 14. We stayed the night at the boarding school in Alassio. I put the missionary crucifix, which Don Bosco and the Pope had blessed, underneath my pillow but forgot all about it until I was on the train. At Buenos Aires I got another one like it and kept on my desk. But for twenty-two years I regretted that loss. What had become of that sacred symbol given to me by Don Bosco? By a wonderful stroke of Divine Providence, the person in charge of the rooms had found it after our departure and asked those of the house which missionary had forgotten it. The young student, Stefano Baracca from Lugo said, "I know it belongs to Fr Vespignani. Give it to me and when I go home for the holidays, I'll have a lovely surprise for his mother." He was true to his word. Mother kept the crucifix as a family heirloom. It was all the more precious because my father had kissed it on his deathbed, my Salesian brother, Fr Stefano held it in his hands during his agony and, finally, mother herself embraced and kissed it before she died. It has now been returned to its fortunate owner who, having had his brother, Fr Ernesto, kiss it in his last agony in Buenos Aires (1926) hopes never to lose it again until he has lovingly kissed it as he himself expires!

Meanwhile, we crossed the border, saying goodbye to Italy, not knowing if we would ever see it again.

Chapter 23

Across Three Countries

It would seem that these memoirs should end at this point which marks the close of my year spent at the school of Don Bosco, yet was not our journey to America the logical completion of that chronological period? In any case it will not displease any reader to learn how Don Bosco's sons travelled in those days; and as far future generations, who knows, perhaps, *olim meminisse iuvabit* [one day it would be a delight to remember].

Having said farewell to our country, we boarded the train and calculated where we would spend the second night of the journey. We then had our first. On consulting the timetable, we saw that we would be in Marseilles at about 10 o'clock that night. Where are we going to sleep? we asked one another. I said to Monsignor Ceccarelli, "The parish priest of St Joseph's Church is one of the best French cooperators. Let's send him a telegram informing him that four of us are arriving tonight." No sooner said than done. We made a combined effort to compose the telegram. We knew very little French, the best in the language was the cleric Panaro, who had worked at Cannes as a boy and spoke some kind of dialect that few people understood. Here is a sample of his French: *Arrivrons quat salesien diz ors* (four Salesians are arriving at 10 o'clock).

This was the telegram, now who was going to sign it? Monsignor Ceccarelli said, "I am not known here, you perhaps." We signed in Don Bosco's name to make sure they would understand. Alas, they understood too well! The train had no sooner reached the station at Marseilles when we heard a shout:

"Don Bosco! Don Bosco!" repeated in various places.

"Look," I said to Monsignor, "that priest is running and calling out Don Bosco's name." At that, the said priest came running up to us and asked panting:

"Where's Don Bosco?" We looked at one another without answering and meanwhile the priest took a sheet of paper from his pocket saying, "Here is Don Bosco's telegram to say he was coming with three Salesians." We were flabbergasted. Fortunately, Monsignor Ceccarelli controlled himself and replied with a certain amount of frankness:

"Don Bosco has had some setbacks which obliged him to stay behind. He has remained at Nice (we had dispatched the hapless telegram from there). He sends his greetings and begs your forgiveness."

In the meantime, a committee of well-to-do gentlemen, who had come to welcome Don Bosco, approached the carriage windows and got ready to give our Father a rousing reception. Picture our confusion! We stood there, suitcases in hand, not daring to descend from the train. We would have taken refuge anywhere! Luckily, Monsignor Ceccarelli looked composed and did all the answering for us. We got down at last and found ourselves surrounded by those good gentlemen who questioned us as to what had prevented Don Bosco from coming. We made a few gestures and left the Monsignor to settle everything.

We found a large number of splendid looking carriages with uniformed drivers outside the station. Everybody waited, watched and then began to learn the disconcerting news. The parish priest had us climb into the magnificent coaches and kept on bewailing the disappointment. "Don Bosco has disappointed me! Oh well, it can't be helped!" At the parish hall we found a new surprise and a much more serious situation.

Another committee of honour, formed of local aristocratic ladies was assembled there. One can well imagine the outbursts of questions: What had happened *en route*? Where was Don Bosco? Why hadn't he arrived? Why had he sent the telegram only a few hours before? We were covered with confusion not knowing what to do with ourselves.

A sumptuous supper had been prepared in the magnificent hall. We were dazzled at the sight of so much pomp, so many flowers, such luxurious settings, and we thought we were dreaming. Oh, that wretched telegram! If we knew nothing else, we at least understood what Don Bosco's name meant in France.

The good parish priest calmed down little by little; the high society representatives had left. Perhaps the worthy cooperator, without a sincere admission on our part, had guessed the grave mistake and did not look for further explanations. We sat down to a sumptuous meal, but we had no appetite. We were then shown to our rooms which were truly princely. As we examined our consciences that night, we found that we had inaugurated our first missionary journey very, very badly. We were stung with remorse at the thought of the displeasure our thoughtlessness might have caused Don Bosco. However, we learned from our mistake, and we truly did learn to be careful when sending telegrams, especially in French.

Very early the following morning Monsignor Ceccarelli and I celebrated Holy Mass. A month commemorating the faithful departed was being celebrated in that church. How many people! How much devotion! How many communions! We went to thank the kind parish priest and, having done our best to make him forget the misadventure, we said goodbye and went to the station.

Since we were anxious to provide for our journey, we bought some Dutch cheese which would come in handy during the days we still had to spend on the train. We didn't risk sending anymore telegrams.

We bought tickets for Perpignan. We settled down in our compartment and when the train began to move, we recited prayers, said our breviary and made our meditation. However, Monsignor Ceccarelli, who was very chatty and good humoured, believed that the best meditation book during long journeys was admiring the beautiful and unusual scenery which the goodness of God has placed all along our way. In fact, he called our attention to everything noteworthy that we saw adding spiritual reflections.

We travelled third class along with soldiers and all kinds of people. We had been given botties of muscatel, but we had no way of uncorking them. We earned friends among the military who uncorked the wine for us and to whom we gave half. Bread and cheese was our food for the first day.

It was evening when we reached Perpignan where we had supper in the unpleasant company of comedians who were at the same inn. We fervently hoped we would not have their company when crossing the Pyrenees. Since there was no railway over those mountains we would have to travel by coach, and by night at that!

There was no shortage of difficulties. It was midnight when we finally stopped and got off at Figueres, the first city we arrived in Spain. When the horses were being changed, we moved away from the carriage to attend to our pressing needs. Suddenly we heard a bell ringing, the cracking of a whip and the grinding of wheels; the stagecoach was leaving! And yet Monsignor Ceccarelli, who had remained near the stable, had told us that we had half an hour. What could we do! In such cases you have to do what you can! We ran at top speed in pursuit of the enormous coach yelling out, but although the driver saw us, he did not stop. Then, taking the opportunity of the coach slowing to go uphill, we grasped each side of it and jumped on. Looking inside, we were surprised to see the comedians, who were urging on the horses and drivers so that we could not descend. It was some time before the three of us could jump to the ground without danger of breaking our bones. Finally, we made our way back to the stable where, panting and shamefaced, we climbed into our own carriage.

Here we found good company. There were four Capuchin Fathers who had come from Ecuador following the death of the heroic President, Garcia Moreno. Their conversation did us much good because, although they presented us with a picture of the American Republics that were in constant revolution and revolt, they edified us by an account of their experiences and apostolic work. We regretted that we had not enough money to invite these good religious to have some supper with us. When it was nearly time for them to leave us at about five in the afternoon, the Monsignor said that since we had to invite them, we would have to make do with just a cup of black coffee without any bread. And this is what we did. At least the coffee warmed us up and served to keep the conversation lively.

We were now to continue our journey by train and thought with dismay about where we would spend the night and obtain some refreshments. But we were on Spanish territory and Monsignor Ceccarelli had greater facility in talking to other passengers. He came to know of a good lady called Dona Maria who lived in Barcelona and who gave hospitality to priests. He took the address and on our arrival in that city, we had someone take us to that hotel. There we found a very kind lady who gave us a warm welcome and offered us lodgings. She immediately took us into a room where about ten priests were sitting around a little altar saying the rosary in Spanish. When the prayer had finished, one of those priests lifted up a little boy to blow out the candles. Quite an original method!

When supper time came (we had not eaten for 24 hours), those good priests, because of I don't know what vigil, told us that since we were Italians and had not taken the *bulla caenae* we could not eat with them, that is, eat meat. A priest then came and asked us if we had the *bulla*. We understood very little Spanish but used what we did know to ask what they meant by this *bulla*. The *bulla caenae*, the *bulla cruzada!* Had we a *bulla?* We didn't have one, but what we did have was a terrific appetite![6]

While all this was going on Monsignor Ceccarelli was explaining to the lady how in Argentina, where we were heading, we had all the privileges allowed in Spain without having to take the famous *bulla*. And so at least, something more substantial was added to the boiled greens which had been served at the beginning. We felt better after our modest meal and as night was falling, we visited some of the beautiful churches of that classic and densely populated city. We continued our journey towards Madrid. Needless to say, as we passed the many places famous for saints and sanctuaries, we reverently acknowledged that blessed land. We passed Monserrate from where some monks who accompanied Christopher Columbus on one of his journeys to America had come. We also passed near Manresa where St Ignatius was inspired to compose his great work, the 'Spiritual Exercises', and to found the Society of Jesus which gave so many missionaries to the two Americas. Such reflections filled us with enthusiasm for our apostolate.

The journey lasted a day and a night as we could not catch all the trains at the right time. When we reached the capital, our dear Monsignor wanted us to see the Royal Palace while King Alfonso XII was coming out solemnly to welcome a delegation. At this very court, our own St Aloysius Gonzaga had once been a page of honour to the Queen. I reflected on this and always enjoyed telling our boys that I had visited the place where the angelic young man had heroically turned his back on the vanities of the world and heeded the voice of Our Lady of Good Counsel who called him to the religious life. We also visited the old and new grave of the farmer St Isidore to whom we recommended our future mission. This memory was always very dear to me because this patron of our agricultural schools was later to give his name to many of our houses and colonies.

---

6   Translators' note: In Spain at this period, all Catholics who bought the *bulla crusada* were dispensed from abstaining from meat on Fridays.

We went to see the Apostolic Nuncio, who was then Monsignor Catania, a native of Romagna and who belonged to the family of the Marquis Catani of Brisighella not far from Faenza. He treated us very cordially and as he spoke, he revealed deep satisfaction at the piety and good character which he perceived in the Spanish people, although he would have liked more of them to receive the Sacraments on the Feast of St Teresa when there were great demonstrations of faith. When the dear Monsignor was subsequently made Cardinal of Ravenna, he kindly told my aunt, Mother Prioress of the Carmelites, and my sister, a nun in the same convent, about the pleasant visit we had had with him in Spain.

We dined as well as we could at the station inn where we wrote letters to Turin. I also wrote to dear Fr Taroni who was so eager for news of the one whom he called his firstborn Salesian, now a missionary of Don Bosco.

We had to make up time in order to catch the ship at Lisbon and hence we made a nonstop journey for a day and a night, having to sacrifice the Sunday. In preparation for this we heard several Masses on the preceding Saturday.

It was early morning when we reached Lisbon. Monsignor Ceccarelli took us to the port, fasting as we were, to watch the sea kingfishers until it was a convenient time to visit the Apostolic Nuncio, Monsignor Sanguigni, with whom he had corresponded by letter from the Curia of Buenos Aires to Rio Janeiro. Here a humorous thing happened to us. We were amazed at our reception. At the Nunciature they were expecting a new Secretary from Rome. When our carriage stopped and priests were seen inside, the Nuncio's household made a dash towards the door to greet us and pay their respects. The first to step out of the carriage was the cleric, Panaro, a good Son of Mary, a bit hastily dressed. They immediately embraced him, calling him, 'reverend secretary'. The poor fellow did not understand what was happening. He drew back saying that I was the secretary. I was, in fact, Monsignor Ceccarelli's secretary. Then they wanted to embrace me and give me the same title. We were even beginning to enjoy ourselves because we finally felt that we would be at home. But there were no more illusions when it became clear exactly whose secretary I was.

The Nuncio was there to give us a warm welcome. He invited us to have breakfast at 10 o'clock not only that morning but every morning. Only Monsignor Ceccarelli could be housed at the Nunciature for the night. The cleric Galluscra slept at the Jesuit house; another cleric and me had a bed in a hotel where neither dinner nor supper was served. Fortunately, we had our Dutch cheese with us! We bought our bread every day from an Italian baker, sometimes spending 200 and sometimes 500 *reís*.[7]

I shall add a detail with regard to these *reís*. Determined to obtain an altar stone at all costs so that we could celebrate Mass on board, we went into a Catholic store where church furnishings were displayed. A gentleman who turned out to be a priest who had studied in Rome (even then, priests did not wear a cassock) acted as our interpreter as we asked for what we wanted. The price was 25,000 *reís*. We renounced our purchase although that handful of *reís* was only equivalent to about 25 lire. The chalice would have cost another 50,000 *reís*. What poor missionaries we were! We realised that you cannot travel without money.

Here a question could arise. Did Monsignor Ceccarelli not come provided with enough money? This was the question we asked ourselves! Probably our good superiors thought the same. He had indeed reached Italy with a full wallet; but he had been generous with everyone. He was not a man to ask anyone for money. The result was that his pockets were now empty, fortunately he found two sterling in the bottom of a bag. However, Divine Providence did not leave us wanting. Our greatest sorrow was that we two priests were unable to celebrate holy Mass, nor could the two clerics receive Holy Communion. Spiritual joy, however, was not lacking. We reflected on St Francis Xavier and St Francis Solano whose apostolic journeys were carried out amid difficulties and dangers while we travelled in comfort.

We immediately set about looking for the agency where we could sign up for our embarkation. Our ship the *Miño* was already in the port. We had to present our papers in order to book a place on board. How would I manage, for I was taking Fr Cagliero's place but had no document bearing that name? The matter grew serious. One more day and three would be setting sail and leaving me behind. I had an idea. On my passport I had the name of the cleric Parte who had stayed behind in Rome with a fever. We are all brothers, all Salesians whether we are called Carlo or Giuseppe or Giovanni; monks and nuns lose their surname. We would go, then, to the consul, tell him about Carlo Pane having remained at Rome and Giovanni Caglieto having been substituted so as not to forfeit the return passage given him by the Government at Uruguay, and see what would happen. As we were climbing the hill to the Italian

---

7   The *real* (plural: *reís*), was the monetary unit of Brazil.

consulate, we recited three Hail Mary's together to Mary Help of Christians. Monsignor Ceccarelli was wearing his official regalia; besides, he was a guest of the Nuncio, the head of the diplomatic corps. In short, our hopes were high. The consul was most obliging. He substituted Carlo Pane's name with that of Giovanni Cagliero, and we, as happy as kings, presented ourselves to the English who, with two or three "yeses" and relative nods admitted all four of us and gave us very comfortable cabins. We were truly satisfied and thanked Divine Providence which had favoured us so wonderfully.

During the three or four days spent at Lisbon we had the sad impression of a city in which the practice of religion was languishing while the very churches offered neither attraction nor incentive to frequent the Sacraments. In some churches you could scarcely detect where the Blessed Sacrament was or find out where to receive Holy Communion. Few people attended the sacred functions. The priests were obliged to wear secular clothes with nothing to distinguish them from lay people. The Nuncio bemoaned this sad situation with us. The Jesuit Chapel had an enclosed yard in front since they were forbidden to have open access to the street. Yet this was one of the most frequented chapels. The lay brother whom the Rector gave us as a guide had been to almost every country in Europe and did not hesitate to speak in any language, earning for himself the title of 'Brother Pentecost'. We chatted for a long time with him, listening to interesting stories which prepared our minds for what Divine Providence might dispose in our regard. We finally said goodbye to our kind hosts including the owners of the hotel who had given us a free bed. We then boarded the *Miño* which was to be our comfortable home for about a month. We began our voyage on November 29, first day of the novena of Mary Immaculate and the eve of the feast of the apostle, St Andrew. An auspicious beginning!

Chapter 24

Crossing the Atlantic Ocean

Having presented our papers to the ship's authorities and duly paid our respects to them we inspected the steamer from stern to stern to become acquainted with our new dwelling. We were comfortable with our four-bed cabin located near the centre. Our fellow passengers included English people (those in command were all English), Portuguese, French and a few Italians, Spaniards and Americans. They treated us very courteous and when they saw that we ourselves showed special marks of respect for Monsignor Ceccarelli they followed suit, always addressing him first and giving him preference.

We had now reached the open sea, leaving the coast further and further behind. The picturesque shores and villages scattered over the green hills had already disappeared. The boat began to rock. We looked at one another's pale faces and felt queasy. I told the Monsignor about my old chest complaint fearing another attack. He himself was not too well either but he made me hurry down into the cabin and lie on my bed. I was just in time. My companions quickly followed me. Truly, we had little experience of the things of this world: those years of great simplicity. I distracted my companions with a tail of my first journey to Alassio when a certain man had told me about a stormy sea voyage during which he had lost all his things, even his hat, when they were near Ancona. He added that everyone threw white things overboard. I thought they had thrown underwear and the like into the sea to lighten the boat. Now I understood what things he meant! For three days there was no better cure for our sea sickness than to stay in bed, reading, keeping each other good company and taking some light nourishment. Becoming acclimatised did the rest. After the first week we were all seasoned travellers.

It is a dangerous temptation to eat vegetables and refreshing food especially south of the Equator. Our cleric Panaro with his big salads attracted the attention of a shrewd Genovese, a certain Rossi, who studied Panaro and teased him with his witty remarks. At table one day, he asked him if he were a priest.

— *Not yet,* answered the good cleric.
— *Let me know when you will be saying Mass.*
— *Why? Do you want to be my sponsor?*
— *Oh yes, that would be an honour for me, a real pleasure.*
— *What present will you give me that day?*
— *I shall give you... a cartload of salad.*

Several years later I met this gentleman in a street in Buenos Aires and he asked me at once if Fr Panaro had said his first Mass. I told him that Panaro was then at Boca and was soon to be ordained and sent to Patagonia. The good man was happy to hear it however he forgot about the cartload of salad which we would have liked. Fr Panaro, however, was determined not to be without a supply of his favourite treat and as head of the Chos Malal Mission in the territory of Neuqucn he cultivated a magnificent garden with all kinds of vegetables and fruits which were, and still are, the admiration of and model for the people of those regions.

We came together several times during the day to pray. There was no lack of fervour but what sadness not to be able to celebrate or receive Holy Communion! We made up for this by reading the Missal. How well I remember that on certain days such as the feast of St Francis Xavier and Mary Immaculate we were flooded with indefinable spiritual consolations by imagining ourselves in the church of Mary Help of Christians in Turin with our saintly Father, Don Bosco. We were dismayed on Sundays to see the whole room decked out with new carpets and the English flag at the head of the table on top of a big cushion. The captain entered to act as minister of worship assisted by his officials who sat around the tables to recite prayers and psalms in the midst of the people sitting on the ground. The sailors, who were nearly all from Genoa, sat with bible in hand, quietly talking among themselves. How could you call really religious those cold exterior actions without anything to uplift the spirit, without the living word of the Church and without true union of hearts? The flag lying there on the cushion showed the official, civil and political character of the assembly. We kept quiet and advised the others to be respectful, but in our hearts, we thanked God for having preserved our country in the Holy

Catholic faith with its Mass, Divine Office, preaching, subject to the infallible word of the Successor of St Peter, the direction of our bishops and priests. In our churches we have adoration of our Sacramental Jesus, prayer before our Sacred Relics, the help given by our veneration for holy images of the crucifix, Our Blessed Lady and the saints. This poor Protestant worship truly moved us to compassion, but we prayed to God for our separated brethren that he might deign to lead them back to the bosom of Holy Mother Church.

Among them there was a young ship's doctor who was particularly deferential towards us and who attracted our attention by his modesty, seriousness and prudence in everything. He spoke to us in Latin, and we understood each other quite well. He liked to join us every day at a game of quoits, draughts or chess. He seemed anxious to tell us that he loved the Catholic religion and would sometimes sit down at the piano and sing the *Ave Maria* with a melodious voice. "This young man will certainly become a Catholic," we said and prayed for him in particular. If he bought some fruit in the ports of call, he would come to Monsignor or to ourselves and offer us a share. He was a good, kind person. This was his first voyage. Let us hope that he had an opportunity later on of getting to know our holy religion well. For us there was the difficulty of language. We were still only potentially missionaries or missionaries in the making.

The steamer halted at San Vicente, a semi-African Portuguese colony. We were appalled by the misery and apparent brutalisation of these people. From there we then resumed our course towards Pernambuco where we stopped for nearly 24 hours under the scorching rays of the equatorial sun. In the distance we saw Olinda which had been spoken of in the news in those days because of the firmness of its bishop in opposing certain laws of the imperial government. It was a firmness which earned him persecution and imprisonment. We continued on to Bahia San Salvador where we stopped for another day. Finally, on December 11, we dropped anchor in the great bay of Rio de Janeiro where we had a three-day rest.

How joyfully we landed and hastened to the palace of Don Bosco's great friend, the dear Bishop Lacerda! We seemed to be restored to new life. We could pay a few visits to Jesus in the Blessed Sacrament, celebrate Holy Mass and were even given a present of the long-desired altar stone and chalice. The bishop welcomed us and would have liked to keep us in Rio de Janeiro to start a foundation there.

We became aware of the great heart of that most worthy and gifted prelate and of his great affection for Don Bosco. After supper the first evening, he made us three Salesians sit opposite him and said, "I won't let you go to bed until you have given me details about what you have seen or heard of Don Bosco since first becoming acquainted with him. Begin now." When I had talked for more than half an hour, he said to another, "He is tired; you continue." The cleric Galbuscra also spoke for a good half an hour. Seeing that he too was getting tired, his Excellency made a sign to the cleric Panaro, the most sparing of words and the most subject to sleep. The good bishop interrupted saying, "I see you are rather tired and sleepy. Stay in bed longer than usual in the morning, we must now talk about Don Bosco. Therefore, let's begin again." I had to start again while the others were falling asleep. He kept us until eleven o'clock and still wanted to hear more. At last, he took pity on us; he let us say our prayers and go to bed.

The next day he wanted to show us around his episcopal palace. When we reached the official reception room where he had been honoured on the day of his episcopal consecration as bishop, he would not go inside but looking behind he said, "You go in. I'm not comfortable there where I received too much responsibility for people. I suffer too much!" We consoled him; he revealed his fears to us. His only support was the thought that Don Bosco had consoled him. This gave him peace.

He then took us to see the huge portraits of his predecessors all around a gallery. He stopped before each one and told the story, events and persecutions, always ending with a *rest in peace.* When he reached the last portrait which was his own, he told us about his life with its contradictions and disillusionments and ended shaking his head, saying, "Never, never will he rest in peace."

He was very pious. He came along to hear my Mass in Chapel, with hands joined and kneeling on the bare ground. He showed great confidence in us, sons of Don Bosco. In the privacy of his library, he revealed his conscience to me as he had done with the Oratory boys at Turin. He was really a man of God harassed with scruples. It seemed that he was too deeply affected by the moral evils of the world; he would have liked to eradicate them all at once. He had an exaggerated desire for the best, mingled with a deep sense of his personal responsibility which gave him no rest. At the same time, he seemed to possess so childlike a simplicity that he was content every time he found someone to whom he could speak with simplicity in the Lord.

Here, too, the brave missionaries had time to do some exploring. His Excellency was determined to open negotiations with us about a foundation. He offered us a country house belonging to the seminary called Jerusuba and situated on the opposite side of the bay about an hour and a half away by steamer. The administrator of the seminary took us to see the house and adjacent wooded land which extended right up to the summit of the mountain. The sun was scorching as we began the climb, and we were very soon in need of refreshments because of our tiredness and thirst. Our two clerics found some woodland fruits most of which were like soft, juicy beans. We ate some and stored up a good supply for the future. When we descended, we learned what we had eaten were seeds from which castor oil was extracted! In addition to this, some good women selling liquor, on seeing us tired and thirsty offered us a glass of brandy which the breathless clerics hastily swallowed. Poor fellows! What a disaster on the journey and on the steamer! The bishop was there waiting for us in his residence, anxious to find out our impressions.

— *Excellent!* We answered. *It is a beautiful place.*

— *I have more faith in the young than in the old. I want to know what these two young men think of it.*

The two clerics writhed, stammered a few words and looked confused.

— *So you didn't like Jerusuba, right?* said the bishop, *tell me truthfully.*

— *Monsignor,* I interrupted, *let them retire. They are overtired and are not feeling very well.*

The bishop wanted to know what had happened, but I told the two clerics to go about their own business. They did so while I sorted everything out as well as I could with the bishop. That day the young missionaries learned a never to be forgotten lesson.

On the last day the bishop wanted to honour us by inviting distinguished people to dinner. He insistently repeated his desire for the foundation of a house in the capital of Brazil. This desire was satisfied a few years later with the foundation of the school at Niteroi, due to the efforts of Bishop Lasagna. He said repeatedly, "We need cobblers, tailors, joiners, masons, we don't need doctors. Let us always pray that there may be fewer doctors and many Christian workers. Blessed be Don Bosco and his work!" When bidding us goodbye he gave each of us a copy of Del Carpio's 'Handbook of Ceremonies' which we kept as a precious souvenir.

We made yet another stop at the Port of Santos and then finally, on Christmas Eve towards evening, we entered the Port of Santa Maria at Buenos Aires. What a memorable entrance! On the first Christmas Eve I celebrated Holy Mass after we two priests had heard each other's Confession and I had heard those of our two clerics. The three received Holy Communion. The year before I had been Don Bosco's deacon at Midnight Mass, and now with that first, unrepeatable Mass I was inaugurating my long-desired mission.

Truly our dear monsignor was over-cautious regarding the private exercise of our sacred ministry. He feared comments on the part of the Protestants. During the celebration of that Midnight Mass, he wanted curtains put up on the little windows of the cabin overlooking the corridor for fear that the lighted candles might be seen. We, on the contrary, were convinced that the authorities on board would not have prevented us from doing for the Catholics what they, in their own way, did on Sundays for the Protestants. How often excessive fear prevents a step being taken, a word being said which would promote more mutual understanding, true freedom of spirit and conscience in everything which the world cannot take for bad even if it does not want to call it good! The fact remains that because that step was not taken, that word not spoken to our kind captain and fellow passengers we were unable to celebrate Mass either before or after Christmas. I said after, because as we had called at the Brazilian ports which were then infected with yellow fever we had to stay in quarantine until the December 28, feast of the Holy Innocents and memorable date of the death of our patron, St Francis de Sales.

After we had dropped anchor on the night of our arrival in the port, a terrible storm arose with a frightening wind which shook everything for an hour and even broke one of the ship's masts. Woe to us had that storm caught us in the Ocean or in the Rio de la Plata which is subject to even worse storms than is the open sea and is more dangerous because of its sandbanks! Our Lady Help of Christians protected us to the last.

During the Christmas festivities the ship was decorated with magnificent carpets and a profusion of flags and flowers obtained at Montevideo. There were nicely painted posters with several religious references to Christmas and with greetings and good wishes. There was a splendid banquet with shared manifestations of Christian joy and cordiality. Oh, how we prayed that night that so many people who, knowing the benefit of the Redemption of Our Lord Jesus Christ, might receive its regenerating Grace and true doctrine by means of union with the one, holy, Catholic and apostolic Church of Rome!

Our dear confrères who had set sail on the *Savoie* had already arrived for the Christmas novena and celebrated the great feast of the Infant Jesus in our three houses and churches of Buenos Aires. They did not know the day of our arrival and disembarkation and so we gave a fine surprise to those at *Mater Misericordiae* on the feast of the Holy Innocents which is usually a day of harmless fun and tricks! We reached the church by the Moreno Road at about 4 in the afternoon and went up into the church. We found ourselves surrounded by young oratory boys who asked us for medals. While we were praying at the altar, they ran off to announce our arrival. Fr Costamagna and others of the house came to meet us and gave us a true, brotherly welcome. We then exchanged impressions of our respective voyages. Our confrères on board the *Savoie* which could be called the 'Salesian steamer' of the first three expeditions, had carried out a most fruitful mission to the benefit of the many emigrants. Their religious practices made in common were attended by passengers of the different classes. On feast days there were solemn services with hymns and music. There were daily catechism classes and lessons in sacred singing for boys and girls given respectively by the Salesians and the Daughters of Mary Help of Christians. Fine serenades with all kinds of hymns and cheerful songs entertained the passengers, all under the direction of the leader, Fr Costamagna. This type of mission continues to this day during our missionary voyages.

Chapter 25

Don Bosco's School Continues

Don Bosco continued to teach us through his letters of which I shall offer some samples. Allow me first to give you some news. I gained my early experience at the Italian church *Mater Misericordiae*. This had been the first home of Fr Cagliero whose fellow worker was Fr Giovanni Battista Baccino. This indefatigable labourer died on July 23, 1877, as a result of overwork in his apostolate. This happened while Fr Cagliero was on his way to Turin and the Archbishop Aneiros was in Italy. I was sent to substitute Fr Baccino to some extent, along with my rector, Fr Costamagna.

From the very outset I was struck by the great affection and sincere attachment of all the local young people for Fr Baccino, that zealous son of Don Bosco. I heard things related which gave me a very high opinion of his zeal, yet he used the simplest and most ordinary methods. On Sundays he devoted his time to the Italians who came morning and evening. He would invite them into the playground after the sacred functions to get to know one another, to build friendships and to talk about Italy, Turin and our lovely customs. He formed a good choir which sang sacred hymns and the Office of the Blessed Virgin. Many young workers assembled for a practice every evening after work. They would recite the rosary with him at Our Lady's altar, chat, sing and play music. In this way he made a large number of good friends who still remember him with gratitude after more than fifty years. Among these friends were two future Bishops, Monsignor Francesco Alberti and Monsignor Giuseppe Americo Otrzali who were still children; several future parish priests such as Father Biasesco of Balvanera the future Director of Salesian cooperators at Buenos Aires: Monsignor Carranza and other future well-known churchmen. From these same friendly religious gatherings came the first Salesian candidates,

Silvestro Chiappini, the two Botta's, Luigi and Enrico, Enrico Rezzonico, Antonio Brasesco and many others who subsequently went to Montevideo or San Nicolas.

Not only did I inherit dear Fr Baccino's dark, stuffy room under the belltower but also his office as vice-chaplain of the church with its clientele for catechism lessons conferences and Confessions. Very soon, however, we rented two little houses where we lodged a dozen boarders and received thirty day students. In March 1878 this school was transferred to the new provincial house of San Carlos at Almagro together with the artisans of Calle Tacuari. The provincial was Fr Francesco Bodratto who was assisted by two vice-rectors, as they were then called, Fr Evasio Rabagliati for the artisans and me for the students which included some candidates.

The letters which I intend to quote for my readers begin from this date. They clearly reveal the concern and solicitude of Blessed Don Bosco to establish and reinforce the regular observance of Salesian life in his first missions for the evangelisation of Patagonia and the Pampas, the object of his dreams.

To Fr Ceccarelli, Mons. Espinosa and Mr Francesco Benitez:
These are three letters in which Don Bosco outlines a plan of action for the Missions entrusted to his sons in America. The rough copy of the plan bearing his signature was given to Fr Cagliero that he might be guided by it in the administration of the first houses at Buenos Aires and San Nicolas. The originals of these letters can be seen in the display cases near Don Bosco's room in which numerous other relics of his are exposed.

1

The Day of the Birth of Our Lord, 1874

Very Reverend Doctor Ceccarelli, Pastor of San Nicolas, Buenos Aires.

May the Grace of Our Lord Jesus Christ always be with us.

The Italian Consul of the Republic of Argentina, Mr Carlo[8] Gazzolo, our friend and benefactor, has told me about your kind letter in which you say you would be glad to have a Salesian mission in your parish. With a truly disinterested charity and zeal, already familiar to us, you offer your house, parish and support to these spiritual sons whom Divine Providence has given me.

Nothing further is needed for the accomplishment of our project since our only desire is to work in the sacred ministry especially on behalf of poor and

---

8   This is a mistake. His name was Giovanni Battista

neglected young people. Catechism, schools, sermons, Sunday recreation areas, homes and schools form our principal apostolate.

I have written, therefore, to the Archbishop to say that I accept the plan and remarked that it would be very useful to have a hostel in Buenos Aires for the reception of our religious who arrive there or have to receive orders or injunctions for the Sacred Ministry. Placing myself in your hands I shall send priests, clerics, lay people, musicians and artisans at the time and in the number which you shall deem necessary. I ask you, however, to let them stay in your present dwelling at least until the newly-arrived have sufficient knowledge of the language and customs for the promotion of the greater glory of God. Who knows, by your example, zeal and advice you may become the actual superior of the Salesians? In short, I beg you to consider us all from this moment as your humble sons in Jesus Christ and to give us all that advice and direction which you deem necessary or opportune for this holy enterprise.

May God bless and preserve you in health that you may continue your work on behalf of your people.

Pray also for me and for all the Salesians. Assuring you of my deep gratitude and respect, I am,

Yours most affectionately in J.C.

John Bosco, priest

2

Very Reverend Mons. Espinosa, Vicar General of Buenos Aires.
May the Grace of Our Lord Jesus Christ be always with us.

Mr Giovanni Battista Gazzolo, the Italian Consul in the Republic of Argentina, has often spoken of the zeal of your Excellency and of the untiring work which you perform on behalf of your vast Archdiocese. At the same time, he has often mentioned the great lack of apostolic workers especially those who are specifically devoted to the Christian education and instruction of the young.

With a view to furthering the spirit of the Salesian Congregation and doing every possible good for the republic which he represents, this kind gentleman decided to write to the aforementioned bishop saying that the Salesians would have no objection to offering their humble services wherever there might be work for them if it were acceptable to him.

Your Excellency kindly replied that the archbishop liked the idea and would willingly receive and protect the new missionaries.

I now express my most lively gratitude to both of you and declare myself ready to accept the proposal. With this in mind I intend to enter into formal communication with you as representative of the Diocesan Ordinary.

We shall be greatly helped in putting this proposal into action by what Dr Ceccarelli, Vicar of San Nicolas has written to the effect that he is ready to offer house, parish and support to the Salesians should they come permanently to work in those many fields which lie barren through want of workers.

The following are the suggestions which I humbly submit to the enlightened wisdom of Your Excellency:

1. I will send some priests to Buenos Aires to set up a central hostel there. It would be very helpful to have some kind of church for the sacred functions especially for teaching catechism to the most neglected boys in the city. The esteemed Mr Gazzolo tells me that it would be very opportune to use the church of Our Lady of Mercy which is about to be vacated. In the absence of a public Church, we could use any premises suitable in some way for gathering and entertaining poor boys.

2. I will then send to San Nicolas the number of priests, clerics and lay people necessary for religious services and singing and also to teach in schools where needed.

3. From these two bases the Salesians could be sent elsewhere in accordance with what the bishop sees best.

If these ideas can be of use for the realisation of our project you could write and let me know and I shall see that they are carried out as soon as possible.

I would like to inform you that our Congregation has been definitively approved by the Holy See. Even though its primary scope is the education of poor youth we are ready to take up any branch of sacred ministry.

Furthermore, the Holy Father, having declared himself our protector, desires that the matter be presented to him before the plans are definitely concluded. I know that this plan will please him very much as he bears a special affection for the distant lands which were the object of his apostolic zeal at the time when he was sent there as Nuncio of the Holy See.[9]

I am also writing to the Vicar of San Nicolas regarding his letter. I have not written to you in either Latin or Spanish because I see that you write very well in Italian.

---

9   He was never Nuncio. Fr Mastai went to Chile in 1823 as observer of the Pontifical Delegate Monsignor Muzzi. They landed in Buenos Aires and left there on January 16, 1824, crossing the Pampas and the Cordillera and reached Santiago on March 17 after unheard of privation.

I recommend myself and my families to your holy prayers and to those of his Excellency, the Archbishop, and sending respectful wishes to both of you I sign myself,

Your grateful and humble servant,

John Bosco, priest

3

Turin, February 2, 1875

Your Excellency,[10]

May the Grace of Our Lord Jesus Christ be always with us.

Many people in the Argentinean Republic and especially Commander Giovanni Gazzolo, have spoken much of your great charity, sincere affection for the Holy See and zeal for everything religious. May God be blessed in everything and give you a long, happy life to the benefit of our Holy Mother Church.

My old friend Dr Ceccarelli has also made particular mention of the special protection which you are so kindly offering to the Salesians destined for the new house at San Nicolas. Sweet stroke of providence! You bear the name of Francesco and are taking the Congregation of St Francis de Sales under your fatherly protection.

I thank you with all my heart and from this moment I will put a special intention for you so that you may participate in all the Masses and prayers that the Salesian Religious will offer in common or in private. Further, every morning at Holy Mass I shall make a special memento that God may grant you a long life.

Since our Congregation is only at its beginning and has in hand the foundation of many houses and schools, we humbly recommend ourselves to your charity for love of Our Lord Jesus Christ.

May God bless us all and grant us all the grace of being able to walk along the path of good and one day be gathered with our Heavenly Father in the abode of the blessed. Amen.

I recommend myself to the charity of your holy prayers and I am,

Yours most sincerely,

John Bosco, priest

---

10   The letter was addressed to Mr José Francisco Benitez, venerable elder of San Nicolas, fervent Catholic and outstanding benefactor of the Salesian Congregation in that country.

4

To Fr Domenico Tomatis

This is a valuable document teaching patience and charity among religious and missionaries. Don Bosco urges Fr Tomatis to bear with a certain difficult character, Molinari by name, a layman and band master. Molinari later left the institute but did not forget his benefactor. In fact, during his last years he sent a grandson to be educated by us. He showed his gratitude in many ways.

My dear Fr Tomatis,

I received your letter and was very pleased that you had a pleasant voyage and that you have the good will to work. Keep it up. Meanwhile, a letter you wrote to [the community at] Varazze has given us to understand that you are not getting on well with a certain companion. This has made a bad impression especially as the letter was read in public.

> *Listen to me, dear Fr Tomatis. A missionary must be ready to give his life for the greater glory of God; should he not be able to bear with dislike for a companion even though he may have notable defects? Listen to what St Paul tells you, "Bear one another's burdens, and in this way, you will fulfil the law of Christ.[11] Love is patient; love is kind; endures all things. Love never ends.[12] And whoever does not provide for relatives, and especially for family members, has denied the faith and is worse than an unbeliever."[13]*

> *So, my dear son, give me this great consolation, nay, do me this great favour, it is Don Bosco who asks for it. In future, let Molinari be your great friend, and if you cannot love him because of his defects, love him for love of God, love him for love of me. You will, won't you? For the rest I am pleased with you, and every morning at Holy Mass I recommend you and your mission to God.*

> *Don't forget the translation of the arithmetic textbook, adding the weights and measures of the Republic of Argentina.*

> *Tell Dr Ceccarelli that I have not been able to obtain the catechism of that Archdiocese and that I would like to have the short one to insert the acts of Faith used in the diocese in the Giovane Provveduto.*

> *God bless you dear Fr Tomatis; do not forget to pray for me who am always in Jesus Christ.*

Your affectionate friend,

John Bosco, priest

Alassio, March 7, 1879

---

11   Gal 6:2.

12   I Cor 13:4,7.

13   I Tim 5:8.

5

To the same person
The tenderness which we find in this letter reveals the great heart of Blessed Don Bosco and his fatherly concern for the good of his missionaries. The letter was brought by the members of our expedition.

My dear Fr Tomatis,

Here are a few lines also for you. I am sure you will be pleased to receive them because they are written by your true friend. You will receive abundant news of us from our confrères just joining you, and from Monsignor Ceccarelli who has seen and whom we have involved in everything. He is very good and kind-hearted.

You too should be, and I command you to be a model in work, mortification, humility and obedience to the newcomers. You will, won't you? I would like you to write a long letter which will be like a rendiconto of your retreat. Tell me frankly about your life, virtues and miracles, present, past and future.

Dear Fr Tomatis, love Don Bosco, as he bears a great affection for you.

I recommend you to God with all my heart at Holy Mass; but pray for me too, who am always in Jesus Christ.

Your affectionate friend,

John Bosco, priest

Sampierdarena November 14, 1877

6

To Fr Giuseppe Vespignani
I had asked Don Bosco to address me in the second person as he did his other Sons whom he had educated as boys; but he answered, "I shall address you in the second person when you behave better." He delayed until 1880.

My dear Fr Vespignani,

I know you are quite well considering your constitution. I know you are working. But on this point go easy; if you want to do a lot, work little, that is, no more than your strength permits.

I want to have detailed news of the hostel, novices, novitiate, study etc.

Your cleric brother is keeping well and is fully determined to be a real Salesian soon and to go and pay you a visit. He gives good hope for the future.

Kindest wishes to Fr Milanesio to whom I shall write as soon as possible. May God bless you with your boys and confrères and help us to fight his battles on earth to be worthy of a crown of glory later on in Heaven.

Fr Nenci is here with us.[14] *His health has improved greatly. He is impatient to go to Patagonia.*

May God bless us all. Pray for me who am in Jesus Christ,

Your affectionate friend,

John Bosco, priest

Turin, August 12, 1878

7

To Fr Domenico Tomatis

In San Nicolas Fr Giuseppe Fagnano had been gravely ill of typhoid and later had to be transferred to Buenos Aires for his convalescence. He held the office of prefect or bursar of the Pius IX College recently inaugurated at San Carlos Almagro. On the May 24 that year, Fr Costamagna had gone into Patagonia therefore it was necessary to send an energetic missionary to Patagónes as rector and another to Viedma on the right bank of the Rio Negro. Fr Pagnano was providentially chosen for Patagónes, while Fr Tomatis who had proved his worth during his internship was nominated rector of San Nicolas. Don Bosco gives him practical instructions. They are excellent counsels for Salesian rectors.

My dear Fr Tomatis,

I have been keeping up-to-date about the events of the school at San Nicolas; presently it seems ready to begin a new phase under your leadership. Good. Courage. We are placing complete hope and trust in you.

I shall give you some advice that I always give to rectors; try to make use of it.

1. Take great care of your health and that of those in your care. See that no one works too much or, on the other hand that no-one is idle.

2. See that you are the first in piety and observance of our Rules; strive to have them observed by the others especially with regard to meditation, the visit to the Blessed Sacrament, weekly Confession, Mass well-celebrated and, for non-priests, frequent Communion.

3. Heroism in bearing with the weaknesses of others.

4. Much kindness with the pupils, giving them every convenience and freedom to go to Confession.

God bless you dear Fr Tomatis, and with you all our other confrères,

---

14   See Chapter 9. pp. 44–45.

boys and our friend Ceccarelli to whom I owe a letter. May God grant health and the grace of a holy life to you all.

Very heartfelt wishes to everyone. Pray for me who am always in J.[esus] C.[hrist],

Yours affectionate friend,

John Bosco, priest

Alassio, September 30, 1879.

P.S. You will gather from my writing that my eyes are much better.

8

To Fr Giuseppe Vespignani
This letter was written a few days after the death of our dear first American Provincial, Fr Francesco Bodratto. I was at his side as vice-rector. The situation was very serious: debts arising from the new foundation, a civil war scarcely over, trouble in the house. We were waiting to hear the name of the new provincial; this explains the advice and consoling words of Blessed [Don Bosco]. For the first time he addresses me in the second person, no doubt to encourage me and show his fatherly trust in me.

My dear Fr Vespignani,

I received your letter with great pleasure. Everything is going well. But now show yourself to be courageous. Patience, prayer, courage: here is our program at this moment. Do everything you can to encourage others and to banish discontent.

Tell the students and our confrères that I am expecting great things from them. Morality, humility, study: this is their program.

God bless you all; believe me in Our Lord Jesus Christ,

Your affectionate friend,

John Bosco, priest

Nizza Monferrato, August 22, 1880

9

To Fr Giacomo Costamagna
In this letter Don Bosco outlines a program for the new provincial of the houses in America. Don Bosco had announced by telegram to the archbishop that Fr Costamagna would be the interim provincial. The definitive election had now taken place as we see from the post-script.

Dear Fr Costamagna,

I have often received your news and your letters. It is serene even though there are some clouds. This is the nature of earthly things. You will receive companions, letters and other things. See about their distribution.

We shall do what we can to settle our common debts and you do the same. I hope that this year things will take a turn for the better.

The need for a Prefecture or a Vicariate Apostolic in Patagonia is very important. The Holy Father desires and recommends it; it is to our advantage. Without it we could not have the support of the Propaganda Fide of Rome, nor of the Propagation for the Faith of Lyons nor of the Holy Childhood. It seems that neither Fr Bodratto nor yourself realise its importance.

You will have news of us from others. I shall limit myself to telling you, "As for you, always be sober, endure suffering ... like a good soldier of Christ Jesus.""[15] But don't forget that we are Salesians, "sal et Lux", the salt of gentleness, patience and charity. Light in all exterior actions "so that they may see your good works and give glory to your Father in heaven."

Give my kindest regards to Deputy Frias, Dr Carranza, and Mr Gazzolo if you have occasion to see him.

May God bless you, all our dear confrères and all our works that everything may be always and only for the greater glory of God. Amen.

Pray always for me who am sincerely in Jesus Christ,

Your affectionate friend,

John Bosco, priest

Turin, [month not indicated] 31, 1881

P.S. Interpret my thoughts and give a little sermon on my behalf to our Sisters.

PS. The General Council has definitively elected you provincial in America. The decree will be sent to you as soon as possible. This is a means of sanctifying yourself and others.

10

To Fr Domenico Tomatis

This is a gentle, gracious exhortation to write and includes valuable counsels. In this as in the preceding letter there is a simple postscript containing the most important item and probably the reason why Don Bosco wrote both letters.

---

15   2 Tim 4:5; 2:3.

My dearest Fr Tomatis,

It is a pleasure for me to have received some letters from you, but they have been all too rare. Your uncle, Fr Tomatis, has the same complaint. Therefore, see to it that once a month I receive news of you and your house.

I know you have a lot to do and this excuses you, I admit. However, the affection that I bear for you makes me really want to be updated about the things concerning you.

I was told that the financial matters of San Nicolas are falling into place. Very good. We will give you the crown of glory when God calls you to heaven.

We still love you here and often talk about you and your poetic prowess. I never forget you at Holy Mass and believe that you too will not forget your old friend.

In particular, I recommend to you the observance of those Rules with which we have consecrated ourselves to the Lord, especially the exercise for a Happy Death.

Tell your boys that I am praying for them and that they should always remember that time is a great treasure and guard against wasting even a second of it.

God bless you, dear Fr Tomatis. God keep you in good health and in His Holy Grace.

Pray for me who am always in Jesus Christ,

Your affectionate friend,

John Bosco, priest

Turin, [no month indicated] 31, 1881

PS. The Superior Chapter has definitively elected Fr Costamagna as Provincial in America. You can pass on the news to those concerned.

11

To Fr Giuseppe Vespignani
Good wishes, promises, counsels, news: always and in everything a most affectionate Father!

My dearest Fr Giuseppe Vespignani,

I have often received your letters with great pleasure. I bless the Lord who has given you sufficient health to work for this universal need. God grant that you may form a numerous band of candidates, professed members and very fervent Salesians for me.

Tell your sons and mine that this friend of theirs in Europe sends advice on how to be happy: fly from sin and go to Holy Communion frequently. You can explain it to them.

I have news that your family is well. Your cleric brother is enthusiastic and wants to become a good Salesian.

God bless you, my dear Fr Giuseppe, and keep you in good health. Pray for me who am always in Jesus Christ.

Your affectionate friend,

John Bosco, priest

Turin, [no month indicated] 31, 1881

12

To the cleric Giovanni Paseri
An affectionate, fatherly letter to prepare him for his approaching ordination to the priesthood. He was a very zealous Salesian and a great worker. He died in 1885. He was the first rector of [the house of] St Catherine, Virgin and Martyr in Buenos Aires.

My dearest cleric Paseri,

You have always been the delight of my heart and now I love you still more because you are totally dedicated to the missions which is the same as saying that you have forsaken everything to consecrate yourself entirely to winning souls. Courage, then, my dear Paseri. Prepare yourself to be a good priest, a holy Salesian. I shall pray much for you but for your part do not forget this friend of yours.

The grace of Our Lord Jesus Christ be always with us, make us strong in temptation and assure us of the way to Heaven.

Pray for me who will always be in the Sacred Hearts of Jesus and Mary,
Your affectionate friend,

John Bosco, priest

Turin [no month indicated) 31, 1881

13

To coadjutor Mateo Sappa, gardener.
A play on his name. He suffered from neurasthenia and accordingly was so upset to see the damage which the ants did to his work that he felt tempted to leave the Congregation! He did, in fact, leave it to enter another religious Congregation and ended up in a mental hospital.

My dearest Br Sappa,

Try, dear Son, to derive your name from "sapere" and not from "zappare" and things will go better.[16] I have often received your news. See that such news is always as good as in the past. Work and obedience will be your fortune.

May God help you to give good example always. Pray to God for me and I too shall pray for you because I want to be always in Jesus Christ.

Your affectionate friend,

John Bosco, priest

Turin, [no month mentioned] 31, 1881

14

To Fr Giacomo Costamagna
The American province was about to be divided. The distance between the houses made this division advisable especially now that we had begun our work in Brazil.

My dear Fr Costamagna,

A few words of heartfelt greetings to you and our dear sons both Salesians and Salesians-to-be.

Fr Lasagna is regaining some strength but is still far from his former robust self. Nevertheless, his desire to be useful to the Congregation urges him to return to the field of action.

He is genuinely good. He speaks well about everyone specially you and this gives me pleasure. Fr Cagliero has written to you for your views on the modifications which seem appropriate in the American Province especially now that we are opening houses in Brazil. I want to follow your opinion in everything.

What is really pressing and awaited with some impatience by the Holy Father is the business of the Apostolic Prefecture or Apostolic Vicariate in Patagonia. I have to give a formal answer to the Holy Father on the opinion of the government and of the archbishop. Has something been done already or is everything still dormant?[17]

---

16   In Piedmontese *sappa* means *zappa*, a hoe or figuratively, toilsome work; and *fare una zappa* means lo make a mistake.

17   Note: The matter was settled in 1883. By a Brief of November 16, Leo XIII divided the immense territory of Patagonia into a Vicariate and a Prefecture Apostolic. By two further Briefs, one of November 20 and the other of December 2, he entrusted the Vicariate to Fr Giovanni Cagliero, naming him Bishop of Magida, and the Prefecture to Fr Giuseppe Pagnano, assigning him the Falkland Islands and Magellan Straits together with Southern Patagonia and Tierra del Fuego.

Give me some positive information which I can present to the Holy Father who desires to take a personal interest in the matter.

I cannot understand Fr Tomatis. He has the obligation of writing to the superior and having others write concerning the personnel of his school. Let me know the moral and material state of our mission as well as the hopes or fears entertained. Without this knowledge we can only go ahead in an uncertain manner. Yet I myself know nothing.

May God bless us all and make as many saints as there are Salesians and may he make a great saint of you!

Pray for me who am always in Jesus Christ,

Your affectionate friend,

John Bosco, priest

San Benigno October 1, 1881

15

To the same
There appears here for the second time the name of the great missionary, Bishop Luigi Lasagna who died in Brazil in a railway accident shortly after his episcopal consecration.

My dear Fr Costamagna,

I entrust to you an undertaking to be carried out. You can get anyone you like to help. Send me the result which I shall communicate to a person who is doing some good for our sons in America.

Our dear Fr Lasagna had a serious operation last Thursday. They were very concerned for two days. He is better now and the doctors have declared him to be out of danger.

The other confrères in Europe are in good health, thank God.

Very heartfelt greetings to all our sons and their pupils in America. Pray much for me because I have serious and difficult matters at hand requiring special enlightenment from heaven.

May God keep us and bless us all in His Holy Grace. Amen.

Your affectionate friend,

John Bosco, priest

Turin, October 10, 1881

16

To Fr Domenico Tomatis
The Italian emigrants of San Nicolas contributed with their offerings to the building of the church and hostel of the Sacred Heart in Rome.

My dear Fr Domenico Tomatis,

I received the generous offering of 12,300 lire which our fervent cooperators at San Nicolas sent to Italy to continue the work of the Sacred Heart Church and hostel in Rome. This offering made by patriotic Christians living so far from us certainly deserved to be mentioned to the Holy Father who entrusted and recommended these buildings precisely to the Salesian cooperators. His Holiness listened with great pleasure to the account, praised the charity of the donors, finally concluded saying, "Thank these dear, good Catholics. I bless them, their families and their undertakings and I grant to all a plenary indulgence to be gained on the day on which they receive Holy Communion."

I am very happy to be able to communicate these kind thoughts of the Supreme Pontiff to these friends and cooperators of ours and I am certain that the Sacred Heart of Jesus, the inexhaustible source of grace and favours will give them a hundredfold in the present life, as our faith teaches, and their real reward in the life to come.

If ever any of these deserving benefactors should come to Italy, I invite them to visit us and consider our Salesian houses as their own.

Greet them very cordially on my behalf and recommend me to their powerful prayers. I shall not forget them when celebrating Holy Mass.

Tell Graziano that I enjoyed his last letter as also that of Fr Rabagliati. I shall answer them and the others as soon as possible.

Fr Lasagna is fully cured and has set out again for Montevideo. His piety and zeal have truly edified us.

The Salesians in Italy, France and Spain have asked me to send their fraternal greetings and recommend themselves to your prayers. Very special wishes and heavenly blessings to Monsignor Ceccarelli.

May the grace of Our Lord Jesus Christ be always with us. Pray for me who is in the Sacred Hearts of Jesus and Mary,

Your affectionate friend,

John Bosco, priest

Turin, December 21, 1881

17

To Fr Giacomo Costamagna

He writes to the provincial in America with the sole purpose of telling him about his audience with the Pope. This, too, is a sign of his deep devotion to the Vicar of Christ.

My dearest in Our Lord,

I give you the consoling news that today, April 25 His Holiness, the Supreme Pontiff Leo XIII deigned to receive me in private audience.

With great pleasure he imparted his Apostolic Blessing to all our confrères, their pupils, and our Salesian cooperators and benefactors.

Make sure to communicate this great news to all those who are interested in our work and who willingly help to promote our holy Catholic Religion.

Pray to God that He may keep us all in His Holy Grace. Recommending myself to your community prayer I have the consolation of professing myself in Jesus Christ,

Your affectionate friend,

John Bosco, priest

Rome, April 25, 1882

18

To the same

The spiritual and temporal prosperity of the Argentinean Province was attributed to this very precious, inspired and timely letter. Certainly, the propaganda which was made of the teaching it contains contributed much towards instilling the good spirit which, from that time particularly, animated all the confrères, priests and clerics as well as coadjutors. Many made a copy or the letter, several thanked Don Bosco for so splendid a document, promising to practise the Preventive System and to avoid all defects opposed to it. Furthermore, those who felt in greater danger of failing in charity and patience bound themselves to it by vow (the fourth Salesian vow, as it were) and renewed this vow every month at the Exercise for a Happy Death.

Dear and ever-beloved Fr Costamagna,

The time of our retreat is approaching, and I who see myself declining in years would like to be able to have with me all my sons and our Sisters in America. However, since this is impossible, I decided to write you a letter which will serve for you and our other confrères as a guide in becoming genuine Salesians, when you make your retreat, which is not long after ours.

First of all, we must bless and thank God who with his wisdom and power has helped us to surmount many serious difficulties which of ourselves we could never have faced. Te Deum, Ave Maria. Secondly, I myself would like to give you all a sermon or rather a conference on the Salesian spirit which should animate and guide our every action and discourse. Let the Preventive System distinguish us. Never cruel punishments, humiliating words or severe rebukes in the presence of others. The words gentleness, charity and patience should resound in the classroom. Never use cutting words or blows whether light or heavy. Let us use healing punishments, always in such a way that those being cautioned become our friends more than ever and they do not go away disheartened.

Let there never be any negative criticism of the orders of superiors but let things which are not to our taste, or which are painful or displeasing be tolerated. Let each Salesian make himself the friend of all and never seek revenge. Let him be ready to forgive, but once he has forgiven a thing let him not bring it up again. The orders of superiors should never be censured and each one should strive to give and promote good example. Let it be inculcated and constantly recommended to all to foster religious vocations as much among the Sisters as among the confrères.

Gentleness in speaking, working and advising wins everyone and everything.

Let this be your plan and that of the others who are to share the preaching in the forthcoming retreat.

Give everyone much freedom and confidence. If anyone should wish to write to his superior or should receive letters from him, such letters should absolutely not be read by anyone else unless the recipient should desire it.

I warmly advise provincials and rectors to give appropriate conferences on the more difficult points. Rather, I recommend Fr Vespignani to be very clear about these things and to explain them to his novices and candidates with due discretion.

I would like as far as possible to avoid any awkward situations in the Congregation after my death. Hence, I am thinking of appointing a Vicar General to be my alter ego in Europe and another one for America. But on this point, you will receive appropriate instructions when the time comes.

It will be very useful if you assemble the rectors of your province a few times during the year to suggest the practical norms I have given above. Read, and encourage the reading and knowledge of our Rules especially the chapter which speaks about the practices of piety, the Introduction which I made to the Rules themselves and the deliberations taken in our general and particular Chapters.

You see that my words will require much explanation, but you are certainly capable of understanding and, where suitable, communicating them to our confrères.

As soon as you can visit his Excellency, Archbishop Espinosa, his Vicars General, Dr Carranza, Dr Terrero and our other friends and give them my humble and affectionate wishes as though I had only each of them to think about.

God bless you, dear Fr Costamagna and with you may he bless and keep all our confrères and Sisters in good health and may Mary Help of Christians guide you all along the path of heaven. Amen
   All of you pray for me.

                         Your affectionate friend in J. [esus] C. [hrist],

                                             John Bosco, priest
Turin, August 10, 1885

19

To the same.
Written from San Benigno Canavese to where the novitiate had been transferred from the Oratory in 1879 under the direction of the first novice master, Fr Barberis.

V.G.M.G.
Oratory of San Benigno Canavese, August 9, 1882.
My dear Fr Costamagna,

I always read your letters very eagerly and we give them an important place by reading them in Chapter meetings. We see the abundant harvest which God places in our hands more and more generously every day. However, we have two obstacles to overcome: scarcity of personnel and the immense work which weighs us down. It seems to me that we can do this: here we will prepare all that is necessary for the usual expedition for the coming year; 1883. In July of the same year, you will come with a companion to pay us a visit and attend the General Chapter which is to take place in August or September.

While you are here you will inspire us all with apostolic zeal and then return to the lands of Cabot with a host of gallant men.

This is only what I am saying here in San Benigno where I have a few moments to spare. Your plans, however; will be formally read out in the Superior Chapter and then we shall agree about their implementation within the limits of possibility.

I am here at San Benigno where we celebrated the feast of St Aloysius yesterday with his Excellency the Bishop of Ivrea who performed all the sacred ceremonies and spent the whole day with us.

The play Patagonia,[18] written by Fr Lemoyne, was presented in the evening. All the people of the neighbouring villages came to this new kind of

---

18   Fr Costamagna had not been present at the first performance (see p.82).

show. There was general enthusiasm and emotion. Everyone wanted to set out for Patagonia.

Please convey my affectionate wishes ta all our confrères. I recommend Fr Debella to you. Take care of him. He can help you do much good, but he needs gentleness and confidence.

I have spoken about you to the clerics and priests of this house. Prolonged applause and greetings from all.

God bless you; God keep you always in His Holy Grace, and with you may He bless Fr Remotti, Fr Bourlot, Fr Vespignani and the others to whom I hope to write some letters as soon as possible.

Also pray for me who is always in J.[esus] C[hrist],

Your affectionate friend,

[Signature omitted]

20

To the same.
This letter overflows with genuine paternal affection. The dream alluded to in the N.B. related by Don Bosco and recorded by Fr Lemoyne, is the one about the future of our missions in America.

My dear Fr Costamagna,

You have gone away, and you have truly broken my heart. I took courage but I suffered and was not able to sleep all night. Today I am calmer; thank God! Here are some pictures for the confrères of our, or rather of your province. We will send them to Fr Lasagna at another time. I am enclosing a letter for Mr Bergasse. If difficulties arise you can count on me without reserve.

Greet Madame Jacques and assure her that the first indigenous girl you baptise on your arrival in Patagonia will be called Agatha.

God bless you, ever dear Fr Costamagna and with you may He bless and protect all your and my dear sons who accompany you. May Our Lady protect you and keep you all on the path to heaven.

Bon voyage!

I am here with a true multitude who pray for you. Amen.

Your affectionate friend,

John Bosco, priest

Turin, 12 November 1883.

NB. You will see the dream recorded by Fr Lemoyne when a few things in it have been corrected.

21

To Fr Domenico Tomatis.
Longing for news, gentle complaints and precious admonitions. He is writing from Mathi near Lanzo, Turin, where he has noticed a big paper mill.

My dear Fr Tomatis,

Since I receive letters from you so rarely, I gather that you have a lot to do. I believe this; but to give news yourself to your dear Don Bosco certainly deserves to be among those things not to he neglected. "What am I to write about!" you will ask. Write about your health and the health of your confrères; whether the Rules of the Congregation are being faithfully observed; whether and how the Exercise for a Happy Death is made. The number of pupils and hopes they give of success. Are you doing anything to foster vocations and what are your hopes! Is Monsignor Ceccarelli still a true friend of the Salesians? I await answers to these questions with great pleasure.

Since my life is rapidly drawing to a close, the things I want to write to you in this letter are those I would recommend to you in my last days of exile, my legacy for you. Dear Fr Tomatis bear well in mind that you became a Salesian to save yourself; preach and recommend the same truth to all our confrères.

Remember that it is not enough to know things, you must practise them. May God grant that the words of the Saviour may not be for us: they say one thing and do another. Keep your eyes on what concerns you. Whenever anyone commits faults or is neglectful, warn him at once without waiting for the wrongs to multiply.

Many will be won over to the Congregation by your exemplary way of life, by your charity in speaking, commanding and bearing with the defects of others.

Constantly recommend frequent reception of the Sacraments of Confession and Communion.

The virtues which will make you happy in time and eternity are humility and charity.

Always be the friend, the father of our confrères; help them as much as you can in spiritual and temporal matters. Learn to involve them in whatever can further the greater glory of God.

Every thought which I express on this sheet of paper needs a bit of explanation. Do this for yourself and the others. God bless you, my ever dear Fr Tomatis. Cordial greetings to all our confrères, friends and benefactors. Tell them I pray every morning for them at Holy Mass and that I humbly recommend myself to the prayers of all.

God grant that we may one day praise the holy names of Jesus and Mary in the happiness of Eternity. Amen.

I shall soon be writing to you personally or through others about other things of some importance.

May Our Lady keep us all firm [in our resolve]and guide us along the path of heaven. Amen.

Your affectionate friend in J.[esus] C[hrist].,

John Bosco, priest

Mathi, August 14, 1885.

Chapter 26

Blessed Don Bosco is Always with Us in Our Mission

The letters just quoted give only a faint idea of Don Bosco's perseverance in keeping close to his missionary sons through his writings. But he also made himself their co-worker, so to speak, using all those ingenious methods which his zeal suggested.

Once, for example, at the beginning of 1883, he dictated a letter to his secretary Fr Berto and addressed it to me in Buenos Aires, "I want to know exactly," he said, "what those boys wish to do to help Don Bosco to save them. This is the mission that God has entrusted to me and to my sons; but I can do nothing unless the boys themselves help me. So you must explain my desire to them and recommend them to be sincere in telling me the means by which they want to help me in this very important matter. Encourage them to be brief but really generous; collect their answers which I shall offer to Jesus in the Blessed Sacrament and to Mary Most Holy, then altogether we shall set about the task seriously, sure of reaching our goal and of being victorious. I greet and bless you all."

This letter aroused great enthusiasm in all our boys who made Don Bosco the finest promises to correspond to the interest he had in them. We had to greatly limit the length of their letters and notes, reducing the contents to the minimum terms. The only one who could leave Argentina that year when the Third General Chapter was held was Fr Fagnano who resided at Patagónes. Blessed Don Bosco greatly desired to talk with him about the missions of Patagonia which were about to be transformed into a Vicariate and Apostolic Prefecture.[19] I went to the Port of Buenos Aires, or rather to the bay where the

---

19   See Chapter 25, letter 14.

steamer was anchored because neither Buenos Aires nor the other capitals had any harbour yet, and handed him the rather bulky parcel of letters. Blessed Don Bosco read them and was very pleased. He then sent a collective answer through Fr Rua and a certain number of little pictures to strengthen the boys in their resolve to help Don Bosco in the great work of their salvation.

That was the year in which separate premises were finally assigned to our candidates. Their assistant, the cleric Mario Migone, had a picture painted for them. It showed Don Bosco explaining his motto: *da mihi ainmas, cetera tolle* to Domenico Savio. Our young Argentineans answered Don Bosco with the same words uttered by the boy from Mondonio, "I understand; here you engage in the business of souls, and I am placing mine in your hands." Happy coincidence! On June 2 [1929], that same historic picture from Pius IX College was displayed on the high altar of San Carlos as an echo of the celebrations for the Beatification of Don Bosco in the Vatican.

Even after his death Don Bosco continued to assist his dear missionaries, I would say personally. I shall relate something of what concerned me more directly.

Speaking about the missions Don Bosco awakened a desire in us for Patagonia and the Pampas not only with his conferences but also with accounts of his wonderful, prophetic dreams. I yearned to go; but first I had to content myself with being a witness to the first expedition of Fr Costamagna and Fr Rabagliati, substituting for them at *Mater Misericordiae* where I was to give them hospitality after their shipwreck on the Santa Rosa. That was from March 7 to May 18, 1878. Later on, at Pius IX College, I catechised the first indigenous person who became the master cobbler at Viedma. Once again, I was to witness the new expedition undertaken by Fr Costamagna with cleric Luigi Botta when they finally reached the Rio Negro precisely on May 24, Feast of Mary Help of Christians, the very special help of the Salesians in that great enterprise.

However, the day of my first longed-for visit to Patagonia did come. It was the feast of the Holy Innocents, 1891, the fourteenth year after our arrival in Argentina when Fr Costamagna summoned me and said without further ado, "As you know, Bishop Cagliero is in Italy and will not return to his See just yet. Fr Migone his Vicar is going to Montevideo on family business and therefore you will go to substitute him. You will preach the retreat to the confrères of Bahia Blanca, to those of Viedma and also to the Daughters of Mary Help of Christians. Go then, to prepare yourself and set out this evening." I packed my suitcase. On my way to the tramcar, I was joined by the provincial himself who wanted to accompany me. During the short journey I asked him, "How long do I have to stay there?" Fr Costamagna with his characteristic promptness answered, "You don't ask questions like that. It may be months, years or even forever."

"Well then," I said, "farewell Buenos Aires!" I caught the night train and was in Bahia the next morning.

During the course of the year, I had suffered from arthritis and had to have a treatment at the thermal baths of Rosario della Frontiera, Salta. My complete cure, however, only came after a novena to Mary Help of Christians which I finished at my new destination on May 24. Work in the school and parish church of San Carlos, together with the fatigue of the exams and distribution of prizes at Christmas, unfortunately wore me out again; hence I fainted while preaching the retreat. How would I get as far as Viedma with two days in a most uncomfortable coach? However, I boarded the so called *galera*, drawn by sixteen horses, the two leaders of which were mounted by people who ruthlessly beat them every time they went into quagmires and dunes so that they might cross them at full speed. On the first evening we reached the Rio Colorado and slept in a kind of inn which we would never visit a second time! We were martyred by *bichucas* or species of hornets which suck blood especially at night.

The following morning was a Sunday and our *galera* resumed its journey. A good Italian, a baker's apprentice on his way to Viedma for employment, made a sign of the cross on arriving at the stagecoach. At this act, our driver, Mora by name, said mockingly, "That's right. We must get ready because we are going to our death!" The joke did not please the passengers, but they kept quiet.

We entered a deep branch of the river and the water had almost reached the seats. The drivers goaded the animals to overcome the current and reach the opposite bank as quickly as possible, but the traces broke, and the horses were detached from the coach. Repairs were made twice with steel wire and leather; and on both occasions in the attempt to advance, the welding gave way. Our brave Mora looked frantically at the horses that had lost their spirit and were standing shivering in the water. As though that was not enough, a fearful thunderstorm broke out and raged so much that we thought it was the end of the world. Thank God the horses made a supreme effort and got us safely to the opposite bank amid the cheers and applause of all the passengers. I then had my revenge by observing to our worthy coachman that in addition to his bravery the sign of the cross made by our young travelling companion had certainly helped us. Then the good fellow, laying aside all his bravado, told us that as a boy he had been in the Confraternity of St Aloysius in the Balearic Islands and he, too, was a Christian. In this way he renewed his profession of faith and religion to the approval of all.

I did not eat all day because I had not foreseen how long the journey would be and had not brought anything with me. At Patagónes the good confrères gave me a simple, joyful welcome, then led me off to rest until it was time to celebrate Mass. I then had something to eat as it was already after midnight. What a pleasure it is to find oneself in the midst of dear ones, in an oasis of friendship and joy, after a long and dangerous journey! It was with true affection and admiration that I greeted those Salesians who shared all the labours of our missions for many years with Fr Fagnano and later with Bishop Cagliero.

When I had said goodbye to these dear confrères, I was taken to Viedma to the central house of the mission and residence of the Apostolic Vicar where they were waiting for me to begin the Retreat that very day. As I was crossing the Rio Negro, I noticed that the boatman had a Romagna accent. He was, in fact, from Sinigallia and had known my paternal grandfather for whom he had worked in the wine business at the Port of Ancona. We rejoiced at this happy encounter, and I spoke a few good words to him to encourage him to attend church and the Salesian house.

At Viedma, too, where nearly all the Salesians of the mission were assembled, I had the great consolation at finding myself among so many confrères who were old friends of mine. They listened to my instructions with much goodness and attention, and all the more so on seeing me suffering from rheumatism which was intensified by the hardships of the journey, change of climate and weariness. Sciatica gave me the most trouble. They were so sorry for me that they wanted to book my passage on the steamer *Pumona* so that I could embark immediately after the retreat. I would not let them do this as I knew I had to keep to the orders of my Superior.

Furthermore, at that time I had a message from Fr Rua that would give me light and strength for the accomplishment of my duty. In January, he had written in the following terms to my predecessor Fr Migone who had asked for a change of place and office. "My dear Fr Mario, you ask me to take you away from the post you occupy, but think about it well: when you have to appear before God at the end of this life would you prefer to leave from the place where obedience has put you or from the place chosen by your own will?" This letter which I had to read as part of my duty seemed to be written just for me; I accordingly resolved not to move no matter what happened. To this situation I attribute the fact which I am about to narrate and from which it will be seen how Don Bosco watches from heaven and assists his sons as they attend to the fulfilment of their duties.

After the retreat I was to say to our own Fr Garone, called *El Doctorcito* because he was the doctor for all those peoples, "I am placing myself in your hands. See if you can heal me of this sciatica and rheumatism." He applied an ointment which made me very weak and caused dryness in the throat and complete loss of appetite. I was unable to take any food for two days. Through the infirmarian Fr Rosmino, the Sisters in charge of the kitchen sent me raw eggs and other light foods, but the nausea was so great that my stomach turned at the sight of them. Once, as l lay in bed I heard the charitable cook, Mother Cassulo, complaining to Fr Rosmino near the serving window about my condition, "But our good Father is really ill," she was saying. "He hasn't eaten anything for days. If he continues like that he will die. So far there hasn't been any priest buried in our cemetery; he would be the first."

When l heard that I called Fr Rosmino and said to him, "Ask that Sister if she still has the bed sheet of Don Bosco that Bishop Cagliero brought back from Turin after having tended our good Father in his last illness; tell her to send it to me instead of talking."

Mother Cassulo who was in the corridor at the other side of the serving window had heard already and was off like a shot to get the precious relic which I put under my pillow. I was left alone to rest and then suddenly, at the foot of my bed I saw Don Bosco, really and truly Don Bosco, with his gentle, smiling face. He was looking at me and opening his hands he said in Spanish, *"Zonzo, por qué no comes un asada concuero?"* [Silly fool, why don't you eat a nice piece of roast beef]. (This is the favourite dish of the Argentineans and country folk). I answered at once: "Yes, yes," and he disappeared.

I immediately summoned Gregorio Mendez, a candidate for the brotherhood, and asked him if he knew how to prepare roast beef. He replied that being a Chilean from the Cordillera, he only knew how to do so in the way used in his country. "It doesn't matter," I replied, "Don Bosco didn't say whether it had to be Argentinean or Chilean. Get the meal and cook it nicely. Meanwhile l shall get up and do as Don Bosco told me. Give me my clothes because I want to dress. Then call the prefect Fr Orsi and the doctor, Fr Garone, to be present at my dinner." At first, they thought I was delirious but seeing my insistence they let me have my way and prepared everything.

I sat down to table with my fine roast beef in front of me in the presence of the two confrères who, astonished at my appetite, gave me a glass of wine as well, the *chacolín*[20] of Viedma and the islands of the Rio Negro. I ate without difficulty and felt so well and strong that I took a walk that evening to the Port of Viedma to welcome a Salesian who was coming from Buenos Aires where the news had spread that I was dying. My sudden cure was complete, and I continued my visit, gave conferences, called on the house at Pringles and went to see acquaintances and benefactors living in that district.

I only returned half of Don Bosco's bed sheet to the Sisters, having first undone the seam joining the two pieces of cloth of which it was formed. I lamely said by way of apology that when you use things, they get smaller; I don't know how convincing my explanation proved. I took that piece of bed sheet which is now kept with the other relics of the Blessed in Pius IX College. In my last conference to the Sisters before returning to Buenos Aires I began by saying, "Notwithstanding the pious desire of Mother Cassulo that I as a priest should inaugurate this cemetery, it seems Don Bosco wants me to take my bones back to Buenos Aires." The Sister protested that she had only meant to emphasise my sorry state.

After the conference, some of the Sisters told me how our dear Father had also appeared on other occasions. Sr Giuseppina Riccardo assured me that once when they were threatened by a violent storm a priest on horseback was seen approaching a group of indigenous people whom he ordered to gather all the cattle in one place while they themselves were to take refuge in their huts. No sooner had they obeyed than a terrible hurricane struck and although it devastated the whole countryside the villagers and their flocks were unharmed. When these people were later shown a portrait of Don Bosco, they said that he was the priest on horseback who had warned them of the approaching danger. It is certain that no other priest could have been there at that time.

I should now conclude the account with my return to the capital, but I want to complete the work by showing how when Don Bosco was alive, he knew

---

20   *Txakoli* or *chacolí* is a slightly sparkling, very dry white wine with high acidity and low alcohol content produced in the Spanish Basque Country, Cantabria and northern Burgos in Spain.

how to make himself present to the missionaries by taking an interest in their families. How could I forget the words he spoke to me in the little boat when we were going to say farewell to the confrères on the *Savoie*? "I will take care of your mother," Don Bosco had said. I was at peace, knowing he meant what he said.

At that time mother was much in need of some good person to think about her and to console her. She suffered from nerves, and this made her more sensitive than ever. Her confessor had not approved of my becoming a Salesian and less still of my going as a missionary to America. Consequently, poor mother had neither spiritual nor temporal consolations from those around her. Furthermore, a few months after my arrival in America I learned from my brothers that she had had a nervous breakdown and only calmed down thanks to a triduum of public prayers and to the comfort given by a venerable priest, Canon of the Count Borrea Buzzacherini, who was to become her new confessor.

But something else also helped her tremendously. In 1898, after an absence of 21 years, I found myself back in Italy for the General Chapter. I went to Lugo to see my mother who allowed me to read a beautiful letter which Don Bosco had written to her from Sampierdarena on the very day I left from Lisbon. I made a copy to keep with me as a precious souvenir of the fatherliness of Don Bosco.

Signora Vespignani,

Fr Giuseppe is leaving, and Fr Giovanni is staying with you in his place. Are you pleased? He is going to America to save souls and to assure the salvation of his own and those of his dear ones.

> *He is at Lisbon; the sea is calm and Mary Help of Christians is covering him with her mantle.*

> > *Be cheerful in God, then, and believe me*
> > *to be your friend in J.[esus] C.[hrist],*

> > > *John Bosco, priest*

Sampierdarena, November 24, 1877

My good mother assured me that this letter had completely dispelled her nervousness and that melancholy to which she was subject in the contradictions and sorrows of this life. The thought that Don Bosco was thinking of her and praying for her and her children filled her with peace and tranquillity. To this attention she also attributed the fact that all her sons and daughters "had taken the right path," as she expressed it. All seven of her children were consecrated to God, four as Salesian priests and three as Sisters, two Daughters of Mary Help of Christians and one Carmelite. Oh, how powerful is the friendship of the saints especially for a mother in the education of her children!

If l were allowed so sublime and divine a comparison, I would almost dare to say that mother's relationship with Blessed Don Bosco was like that described in the Gospel: "the disciple took her into his own home" (Jn 19:27). It really seemed as though Don Bosco considered her as his own mamma Margherita since he arranged for her to come to Turin and offered her a place in the house at Mathi with other mothers of Salesians. She later entered a home for ladies in Giaveno run by the Daughters of Mary Help of Christians and finally brought her days to a holy end in the house at Sassi on November 24, 1900. At the time we were in Buenos Aires celebrating the Silver Jubilee of our missions with Fr Albera who had been sent to us as extraordinary visitor by the successor of Don Bosco.

To complete my account, I shall add the following singular event. On November 21, I had closed myself up in the college library preparing the 'Report on Salesian Cooperation in Argentina' to be read at the conference, when I heard painful breathing like a death-rattle for more than half an hour. I got the feeling at once that mother was about to leave us. My brother, Fr Pietro heard the same thing. We recited the prayers for the dying, uniting with the other members of the family who surrounded mother in the rest home at Sassi, near Turin. Allow me to say that those who approached us while this phenomenon was taking place were not aware of anything unusual. "It was a strange case of telepathy," they said. Then a distinguished Salesian cooperator out here sent a cable to Turin without my knowledge, asking for mother. It was announced at once that she was "gravely ill but still living". They wrote to tell us that they had told her about the telegram, she smiled and sent us her blessing. We then received the news of her holy death.

Chapter 27

Portrait of Blessed Don Bosco

People have tried to portray Don Bosco in many ways with photographic skill as well as with a paintbrush, but portraits are never exactly the same as the original. In 1876 I found a photograph in the little library of the school at Alassio showing Don Bosco with an open book in his hand. I studied it on my journey to Turin, but I would not have recognised him when I was actually in his presence if Fr Celestino Durando had not pointed him out to me and said, "There he is". It was the same with his moral and spiritual countenance and it was difficult to form an adequate idea of his personality. Still, having shown the school of Don Bosco in action I would like to attempt at least an outline sketch of our teacher, using my personal recollections, and drawing from the impressions and judgment of others.

ONE

My first idea of Don Bosco

Before I saw Don Bosco and lived with him, I had read his pamphlets written for the *Letture Cattoliche* and I was familiar with the *Giovane Provveduto* which we used in the Seminary. However, on the day of my first Mass, I had heard the things narrated at table by Fr Francesco Cerruti to the guests who were mostly priests. Fr Cerruti painted [a portrait of] him as an educator of the young, full of zeal for the salvation of the most abandoned and misguided young people. He told us how all of Don Bosco's conversations invariably ended with some reference to spiritual things and to eternal salvation. He related Don Bosco's recent meeting with the ministers Depretis and Zanardelli in the school at Lanzo when the railway was being inaugurated. He spoke of how he had gradually suggested the idea of their returning to God through confession and how they had expressed their satisfaction and gratitude before leaving. We knew that Don Bosco was a saint, but we did not realise how great he was.

Our parish priest, Fr Cavina, was very eager to know how Don Bosco had formed the Salesian Congregation because he dreamed of imitating him in a small way. Therefore, he had endless questions. Still, we were very far from having a complete picture of him.

Soon afterwards, however, all these ideas which kept going around in my head suddenly took definite shape and helped me to discover the real Don Bosco. I have already said that I took my three brothers and four other boys from Lugo to Alassio in 1876. I was making my meditation in the sacristy on Martha and Mary from a book by the Jesuit Avancini (Monday and Tuesday of the 22nd week after Pentecost). Here I recognised the lovable image of Don Bosco and his Salesians devoted as they are to a life of piety and work, and intent not only on practising this kind of life but also on teaching it. All the texts quoted in those two meditations gave me a description of the personal and apostolic life of Don Bosco and his sons. For example, St Bernard said of Mary that by sitting and listening in obedience to the Master, she was prepared for anything. The author also takes inspiration from the Gospel regarding Martha's activity in performing her household tasks to describe community life in a religious family. Then there was the complaint of Martha about her sister and the correction administered by Jesus in connection with the anxieties and temptations of an excessively active life. Finally, there was the *one thing alone is necessary*, as though to say that one dish is enough, that there is no need of many things for the body and that preference must always be given to spiritual things. In this I saw the temperance and generous, joyful poverty of the Salesian life.

I rose from my meditation as though I had seen the genuine portrait of Don Bosco and his pious Society and having celebrated Holy Mass while under such an impression, I felt I was a Salesian myself. That is why I went to the rector, Fr Cerruti and said to him, "I am going to Turin not merely to see Don Bosco but to stay with him. I think I understand what his Congregation is and the nature of Salesian life. Please give me a letter of introduction for Don Bosco." I left Alassio not only with that paper portrait in my pocket but also with my mind deeply imbued with the genuine portrait of Don Bosco which Jesus himself had drawn for me in his Holy Gospel.

Two

Don Bosco, according to Cardinal Cagliero

When Bishop Cagliero was with us in Argentina, we asked him again and again to give us a good description, a natural portrait of Don Bosco in the early years of his priesthood when he himself had known him at Castelnuovo and then in Turin. I personally wanted to know how they saw his sanctity increase and become gradually manifest. This was the bishop's reply, "We always found him the same, to us he seemed perfect and holy, full of love for God and souls. He had by this time reached the maturity in his holiness, possessing all the virtues which he spread everywhere around him by word and example and especially by unceasing zeal and charity towards the most needy."

This concise answer pleased us but did not satisfy us. Therefore, we multiplied questions on this or that thing in particular. The bishop took every opportunity to explain and make applications of the characteristics of piety, charity, spiritual direction, Preventive System and fatherliness or amiability of Don Bosco. From this one could understand that our Father had a special way of thinking, working and directing which was quite distinct from all other saints and founders. Indeed, Cardinal Cagliero never grew tired of repeating in his conferences and conversations to the confrères and still more to those directing the houses and works, "Be careful not to follow the crowd, i.e., do not worry about what others do, trying to imitate methods, systems and other customs proper to various countries other persons or religious communities. Let us all propose one single model for ourselves, one teacher, one Father."

We had just preached a retreat together to the pupils of the College of Mary Help of Christians. This was a school recognised by the State which had already formed a numerous band of women and men teachers who were exercising a real apostolate in the government schools. We were having supper alone at a very late hour on the last evening. Noticing that the bishop appeared rather restless, I asked him if he were tired after all the preaching and confessions. He replied with his typical vivacity, "A son of Don Bosco is never tired of preaching or hearing confessions. But, my dear friend, these people are greatly in need of spiritual direction as they are exposed to many dangers, like lambs among wolves." Striking the table with his knife he repeated, "Direction! Direction! But as Don Bosco taught it to us: to guide souls, sustain them with the holy Sacraments, give them a longing for Holy Communion, keep them united to Jesus in the Blessed Sacrament and to Mary Help of Christians.

Do you understand?" I would have liked many others to have witnessed this apostolic outpouring of the dear bishop in recalling the spiritual direction of his great Father, Don Bosco! It was an unforgettable lesson for me.

This eminent son of Don Bosco never lost sight of his Father's image to which he habitually referred especially when making important decisions or setting about new works. We experienced this not only in his high office as Don Bosco's Vicar for all of America but even more when he gave conferences and heard our confessions. Expressions like the following sprang from his filial heart. "Don Bosco said such and such, Don Bosco did such and such; Don Bosco taught us to behave in this way, to deal with people in this manner." Furthermore, if I may be allowed, for the sake of edification, to express an idea which I formed of him when he was in the missions and we heard each other's Confession, he always compared his own conduct with that of Don Bosco and wanted others to do likewise at the examination of conscience and in Confession. He would tell us, "Don Bosco was always united to God; he guided all to God. His talks always ended skilfully with a thought on God or salvation. Don Bosco was even-tempered; he was always the same. He always treated everyone amiably, and always did as much good as possible to everyone. So must I, so must you, so must all of us."

With this picture of Don Bosco among his boys at the Oratory, both boarders and day pupils constantly before him, he would visit the schools. If he noticed that discipline was rather rigid, that relationships between the rectors, confrères and pupils were not personal and friendly, in short if he did not recognise Don Bosco's Oratory in a house, he would immediately make his observations to the prefect, counsellor for studies or rector. He would give a few sweets to the teachers and assistants recommending gentleness, amiability, pleasantness and use of the means suggested in the Preventive System and summarised by the words, pure and patient love. So it was that when addressing the confrères, young pupils, past pupils or cooperators he never failed to draw a living picture of Don Bosco in his Oratory among his boys and entirely consecrated to their spiritual and temporal wellbeing. We were convinced that when Bishop Cagliero saw the schools of Argentina again in 1885 and noticed some deviation beginning to take place, he urged our Father to write the letter dated August 10, reproduced above, and addressed to the provincial, Fr Costamagna. In this letter Don Bosco not only formally recalls his method but clearly defines his spirit, since some were moving away from certain aspects of it. The letter worked wonders among his sons in America who even went so far as to make a vow, as we have said, of faithfully practising its prescriptions and counsels.

THREE

Blessed Don Bosco in the mind of the Holy Father Pius XI

In his discourses on the virtues, miracles and works of Don Bosco given at the time of the beatification, the Holy Father Pius XI has given us a wonderful picture of our saintly founder. On re-reading its salient points one has to agree with Fr Francesia. When he heard someone read how the Pope, when giving a medal of Don Bosco to workers after having called Don Bosco "a great worker" and "the creator of an immensely beneficial and well-thought-out work",[21] Francesia exclaimed, "What a noble expression! How true it is that great people understand one another!" The Pope showed that he really had understood Don Bosco immediately from his first personal contact with him.

The first picture presents us with a prelude to what the Sovereign Pontiff would say in three successive discourses. In 1922 he said to the boys of the Sacred Heart Hostel in Rome, "It is our deepest pleasure to know that we are among the oldest personal friends of Venerable Don Bosco. We have seen this glorious father and benefactor of yours. We have seen him with our own eyes. We were closely united to him. There was a lengthy, in-depth exchange of ideas, thoughts and reflections between us. We have seen this great giant and promoter of Christian education. We have observed him in that modest position which he took up among his dear ones and which was at the same time an eminent position of command, as vast as the world and also as beneficent. We are therefore enthusiastic admirers of the works of Don Bosco, happy to have known him and to have been able to help his work by our modest contribution."

On February 20, 1927, the Sovereign Pontiff expanded upon the decree on the heroicity of Don Bosco's virtues as follows:

> He was endowed with strength, mental vigour, a warm heart, with an energetic hand, with outstanding power to think, to love, to work; with thoughts which were full of light, grandiose, deep and certainly not ordinary thoughts, but rather superior by far to any ordinary thought; he had the mental agility and intuitiveness proper of those geniuses (and this is generally not well known or noticed) who could be categorised as real genius; he was a genius who easily could have had success as a scholar, as thinker or as a writer. ...It is here [spreading popular literature] that you can detect the outstanding and elevated brilliance of his thinking which laid out for him the steps of that great work with which he would

---

21   *L'Osservatore Romano*, lunedi-martedi, 4–5 nov, 1929.

first of all fill up his life and then the entire world. It is there that you can find that first invitation, that first tendency, that first display of this powerful talent; the task of spreading printed material through the press and bookstores were the works he most loved. This we have also seen with our own eyes. This we have heard from his lips. This was what he was most proud of. He himself said to us, "Don Bosco (he always spoke of himself in the third person) always intends to be in the vanguard of progress in these things," and he was speaking of publications and of printing presses.

The golden key to this wonderful, infinitely precious mystery of his great, fertile active life, to his invincible energy for work, to his indomitable endurance under a daily strain which never slackened, hour after hour, from morning until night, from night until morning, whenever such a strain was necessary (and it often was), lay in his heart, in the intensity and generosity of his feelings. The magnificent words 'God gave him very great wisdom, discernment, and breadth of understanding as vast as the sand on the seashore' [Kgs 4:29], could very well apply to him; in fact, they seem as though they had been written for him, as well as for other great heroes of charity and of charitable works. Now, 40 years after his death look at his works! They are scattered all over the world, on all shores, even 'as the sand on the seashore'. ...Here are the sons of the Pious Society; here are the Daughters of Mary Help of Christians; here are the professed religious, the novices, and the candidates; they are already 16,000—and perhaps even more at the moment in which we are speaking—workers of this huge, magnificent undertaking. ...It is even more comforting to reflect on the fact that all this magnificent and miraculous expansion can be traced directly back to him who continues to govern everything, not as a father who is far away, but as the ever-present Founder who remains active through the eternal vitality of his teachings, in his method of education and above all in the example he gave! His example! Beloved children, these are the most beautiful items, if not the only useful items, of today's great feast. ...Not everyone is given the same amount of grace; not everyone is conferred with the grace to follow clearly lit pathways, and yet how open are his examples to be imitated by everyone, as it has been opportunely pointed out in that life so active, so recollected, so operative and so much involved in prayer.

This, as a matter of fact, was one of his more beautiful characteristics: he was always present for everything; he was involved in a multitude of works, always pressured by problems, always engaged in checking on requests and in consultations, and yet his spirit was always elsewhere, always uplifted where his serenity was never disturbed; where calmness reigned supreme, and he was always in control. This is the way by which in Don Bosco work was indeed as effective as prayer. This is the way Don Bosco carried out the great principle of the Christian life: the one who works, prays!

This was, and should always remain, the great glory of his sons and daughters! What great merit there was in that life, forgetful of itself, only to dedicate itself to the little ones, to the most humble and to the least attractive aspects, if we may so describe them, of human misery! ...At any rate, by looking at Don Bosco and his undertakings, we can all think about and reach this conclusion: while it is true that we cannot achieve what we would want to achieve, yet we can all decide to attain what we can really attain.

In this second discourse when the decree was being given on our founder's miracles, feast of St Joseph, 1929, the Holy Father added further reflections on the virtues of Don Bosco:

In the wake of an event for which the whole world today rejoices and shall continue to rejoice for some time to come and joins with us in giving thanks to God for it, there comes the proclamation of the miracles of Don Bosco, of this faithful and wise servant of Christ's Church, and of this Holy Roman See. Indeed, as we ourselves heard him say with his very own lips, the solution of this deplorable dispute was always uppermost in his mind and in his heart, but in a manner suited to so wise and faithful a servant, meaning that he did not desire any kind of solution whatsoever, as so many people had imagined, interfering with and confusing the issues, but a solution such as would, first of all, protect the honour of God, the prestige of the church, and the welfare of souls.

For this was one of his most striking features: his absolute calmness, his good use of time, that enabled him to attend to everyone who turned to him with such tranquillity, as though he had nothing else to do. This was one of his striking traits, and not the least one, which we had occasion to admire in him. To this we would add the gift of prophecy.

Where did the Servant of God find the strength to accomplish so much? There is a secret, and he, himself, revealed it continuously, perhaps without realising it. This secret is hidden in a phrase that he had often used and which he took as the motto of his entire life *Da Mihi Animas Coetero Tolle*, give me souls, take away the rest. Herein lies the secret of his great heart, of his strength, of his burning charity for young people most in need, whom he loved the most, whom he first began to help, and whom he continues to assist even now. *Da Mihi Animas!* Yes, Don Bosco loved the young because he loved Our Lord Jesus Christ, and therefore he looked at them from the viewpoint of the heart and blood of the Redeemer. That was why no undertaking was ever impossible for him; no treasure was too precious to contribute it to the salvation of others.

The Pope drew yet another deeply beautiful and consoling thought from the wonders of Don Bosco's life: the fidelity of God towards his humble, faithful, generous servant:

How beautiful, how comforting, how stimulating, is the thought of God's sovereign fidelity to his servants! This is the truth; this is the most beautiful and sublime light, which surrounds Don Bosco today this humble, faithful servant who was a mere mortal, a humble servant of God who spared no effort so that he might serve God generously, he was a poor man in the eyes of the world. Yet, lo and behold! God opens the heavens, and His voice resounds unto the remotest corners of the earth, with the strength and splendour of his miracles. Today, before our eyes he lifts the stone which covers the glorious tomb and calls forth his faithful servant to a truly glorious resurrection. ...Don Bosco has really proclaimed God before humankind by his whole life and by the work of the Institutes which have continued his activity, and now God recognises and glorifies him before the whole world.

In his *Tuto* discourse a short time before the Beatification, the Pope added some more colourful brushstrokes to the sketch of Don Bosco relying upon his own personal knowledge of him:

Furthermore, this old acquaintance of ours (we could say), our friendship with Don Bosco, even though we were at the beginning of our priesthood and he was about to reach its sunset, this priestly friendship of ours which makes him come alive in our heart with all the joy, cheerfulness, edification provided by his memory has been reawakened during these days and these hours. It is now that this figure, the great Servant of God, appears on the horizon, not only of this country but of the entire world. It is now when particular and solemnly important events have been recorded in the history of the Holy See and of the Church and of this country. We must remember, with our knowledge of the facts, that Don Bosco was one of the first, eminent, and respected men who deplored the systematic tampering with the rights of the church and of the Holy See, who lamented that those who govern the country were following pathways which were practically impossible to walk on without trampling upon the most sacred rites of the Church. Don Bosco was among the first people who appealed to both God and humankind so that a possible remedy be found for so many troubles, so that a possible solution be found in order that the sun of justice might again shine and provide serenity for human spirits. Divine Providence leads him, proposes him, to the fullness of sacred honours exactly in these hours and in the wake of events that he himself foretold. Don Bosco's beatification will be the first that we will joyously proclaim before the world after these events. There is nothing we can do but give thanks, and wonder. What is there for us to fear, what is there that we may not venture to hope and trust, with certainty that we will be graciously heard?

Finally, in his discourse of the July 3, 1929, during the solemn audience in the courtyard of St Damasus, the Holy Father expressed these ideas:

Beloved sons, we congratulate all of you; no matter what assignment you hold, what responsibility and rank you have, however humble it may be, in this mighty family, in the mighty army, in this powerful concordance of goodness and truth. When we think about the value of an individual's Christian education, a Christian education envisioned by Don Bosco—deeply, completely exquisitely Christian and Catholic—when we think about this treasure multiplied by people who can multiply so abundantly, we experience a truly joyous exultation and gratitude to God who knows how to create such works and keep them alive in this world, in this wretched world where the attacks of evil against all that is good, against Christian truth, go on relentlessly.

Yet you must understand that the genuine glory of Don Bosco in this world lies in your hands; it depends on you. The words that we utter are not our own but they are the words of God: *Gloria Patris filii sapientes* [wise children are the glory of their father].

Your father will be glorified with the finest glory that humanly speaking can be given to him, if you will be wise children of such a father, if you will be able to know, as you do now, and as hopefully you will be able to understand in the future and in an even better way, Don Bosco's spirit, the spirit of his work; if you will be able to continue his work with his spirit ever better, just as he desired, without measuring the amount of work needed, without measuring the amount of dedication needed, but instead without measuring the amount of unselfishness demanded of you as a person as long as it contributes to the good of others. We feel we almost see him as we say all this. We still remember what he used to say is a glorious ideal to live by; anyone who doesn't work is not a Salesian. We ourselves still recall the beautiful words that he uttered to us as he was looking to the future with the intuitiveness of a genius—when we congratulated him on having seen so many marvellous things in his houses, in his workshops, in his classrooms, and mind you, it was not a question of stressing what was good in itself, but only the structure within which the good could emerge, the structure which he followed with the certitude produced by successful inspiration. As you know, when obliged to speak about himself he always did so in the third person, and when we thus congratulated him, he answered, 'Whenever the mighty cause of goodness is involved Don Bosco wishes to be in the vanguard of progress, at all times.' ...this will be your watchword, and it should always spur you on to advance courageously along the pathways opened up before you by the words, the exhortations and the examples, and now by the intercession of Blessed John Bosco.

Chapter 28

Final Words on the Spirit of Blessed Don Bosco

In his discourse after the reading of the Decree of the heroicity of Don Bosco's virtues, the Holy father Pius XI recalled personal reminiscences of nearly half a century before. He not only described the activity of our saintly founder but also investigated its cause, origin and reason which he traced to his spirit of generosity and charity towards God and others. Those who were fortunate enough to be present on that occasion were deeply moved, and especially those who could repeat with the Pontiff, "We have seen him, we have heard him and bear his true image, his clear-cut and indelible spiritual features within our minds and hearts." It was precisely among these first sons and disciples of Don Bosco that the lively desire then arose of seeing a genuine reproduction of the real Don Bosco, of the whole of our Don Bosco such as we visualised him in ourselves. We had contemplated him in his various loveable and admirable attitudes at the time when we had the enviable fortune of approaching him in his room, in church, in the whole Oratory, in the confessional, being able to see him in the pulpit or on the platform as he gave his Good Nights and especially at the altar of our Sacramental Lord or before his picture of Mary Help of Christians.

The result of this desire was that we gathered together in Rome and Turin for some familiar conversations in which we, who had known him in those early days asked ourselves what distinguished Don Bosco the most, what was his dominant virtue; in short, what was the characteristic note of his spirit? Some said it was purity expressed in composure and modesty in all his words and actions. Some others said it was gentleness and amiability in dealing with everyone, especially the humblest and poorest. Another said it was unchangeable serenity and a fatherly eye which made no distinction of persons. Still another said it was indefatigable zeal for the salvation of young people together with invincible zeal in founding new charitable works and in thinking out new means of exercising the apostolate. But after we had all said our bit we realised, like the Queen of Saba with regard to Solomon, that we had spoken all too inadequately that we were just speaking falteringly about the spirit of Don Bosco which we would have liked to define and present as a personal memento to our pupils, confrères and cooperators. We ended by repeating the Holy Father's thought: God gave him a heart as wide as the sands on the seashore. It is impossible to grasp and estimate the immensity of the acts of piety, charity, gentleness, patience, generosity and sacrifice which sprang from the heart of Don Bosco and spread throughout the world.

"It doesn't matter," said one of our company, "let us study the spirit of Don Bosco, following the example given us by the Church in the course of the canonical process and let this be our plan: to call upon the evidence of our personal recollections and of those who were privileged to live for some time with our Blessed Founder, then bring together the evidence of many authoritative Salesians. Finally, we will bring the characteristic traits of our dear father to life in ourselves and to help cooperators and past pupils to be enthusiastic about Don Bosco and eager to imitate his spirit of prayer and charity particularly towards poor and neglected young people. Do you not think that Don Bosco concentrated the whole of his personal and apostolic life in these two virtues?"

"Yes, but still," observed others, "so far this spirit of Don Bosco has not been well described. Who has fathomed his interior life, a life of prayer and contemplation, a life of fidelity to grace, a life rich with the gifts of the Holy Spirit? Struck by his extraordinary activity, orators and writers have brought his works into relief without delving far enough into the motivating secret of all his action."

The difficulty of making a complete definition of the spirit of Don Bosco, the timeliness of a reproduction of his piety and charity, the wish that the central fire, as it were, which radiates the great light of good works might become more and more brilliant: these were the three points around which the august words of the Holy Father revolved. But if the Pope's discourses recall the general attention to matters on which at first the need had hardly been felt of reflecting seriously, it does not mean that we have no authorised and, I would say, official definition of the spirit of Don Bosco. Here, if I may, I shall relate an incident.

General Chapter XII held at the Oratory in 1922 had given the new Rector Major, Fr Filippo Rinaldi, and his General Council the work of revising our regulations according to special criteria already expressed in preceding General Chapters and then reconfirmed. Among the Regulations to be revised was that concerning the novitiates, because it was supremely important for our novices to have an exact definition of the Salesian spirit with which they were to be imbued. "What was the mind and heart, what was the soul and life of Don Bosco?" asked those who were revising the Regulations. There was indeed a great need of serious reflection in order to give a good definition of that spirit of Don Bosco which, with God's grace, had to be transmitted to all the candidates to the Salesian Society. Our Constitutions already contained various references to the spirit proper to a Salesian, especially in Article 180 which says, "If the novice shows, after his year's novitiate that his aim in all things is the greater glory of God and is imbued with the spirit of the Society, and if he has been exemplary in the practices of piety and the exercise of good works, his second trial can be deemed completed." But the question as to what the spirit of the Society was still remained.

This was precisely why our Rector Major recommended a serious study of the subject to his chapter members. The principal duties of the novices having been reduced to three headings, he himself, following special prayers, closed his explanation by declaring it obligatory for the novices, "to strive by constant vigilance and persevering work on themselves... to acquire the virtues necessary for a good Salesian and that untiring work sanctified by prayer and union with God which should characterise the sons of Don Bosco." Having thus expressed his thought, he desired every member of the Chapter to reflect in his own time on this concept and to put a special intention at Holy Mass the following day to obtain enlightenment from the Holy Spirit. On the following day each person declared that no better definition of the Salesian spirit could be made. Hence the above-mentioned definition of the spirit of Don Bosco and his sons was approved. This definition was solemnly confirmed by the Holy Father Pius XI in his discourses of February 20, 1929. "How much there is for all to imitate in that life which was so busy and so recollected, so active and so prayerful! Indeed, one of his finest characteristics was that of being present to all, endlessly busy among crowds of people, with business matters, with a host of requests and consultations, and yet always elsewhere in spirit, always in the presence of God, where serenity was undisturbed, and tranquillity reigned. The result was that his work was really effective prayer; really proved the great principle of Christian life: the one who works, prays!"

Chapter 29

Reminiscences and Impressions

To tell the truth, all the preceding chapters together form a network of personal reminiscences. But here in this penultimate chapter I propose recalling some in particular which did not fit in elsewhere and which were linked to lasting impressions.

One thing which struck me from the beginning in Don Bosco was his manner of dealing with boys wherever they approached him. There was never such a thing as a worldly or sentimental embrace! He barely allowed himself to place his hand lightly on the head, by way of blessing as it were. Furthermore, he had a way all his own of looking at his boys. I am not speaking only of the purity of his look which was directed to the immortal soul destined for heaven, but also of his deeply intuitive look which very often saw clearly what the future held for each person. We ourselves would eagerly try to make him reveal the future, and he with a smile and a joke, would sometimes utter real prophecies which time confirmed.

Another thing which greatly impressed me at once was to see how all the members of the house could go to speak with Don Bosco at certain times of the evening and how this was a great means of keeping them happy and cheerful. That confidence, above all, and those heart-to-heart talks served as support in difficulties, help in their perseverance, and in the fostering of many fine vocations.

While on this point I would like to observe that Blessed Don Bosco maintained a dual type of relationship with his pupils. The first was spiritual, that of a confessor and penitent, although at the Oratory there was complete freedom to choose any confessor, and the second was paternal or friendly, between superior and dependent. These two kinds of relationship alternated in such a way that it could well be said that Don Bosco's sons were in continual communication with him from morning till night: in church, on the playground, in their occupations, at study and at school and that everything was governed by this father himself according to his method. At least once a month he was handed the marks of the pupils who always and everywhere flocked around him for a word or a smile, to kiss his hand, showing him their lively desire to please him and to correspond with his care of them.

Positive and practical as he was, Don Bosco handed his youngsters the *Giovane Provveduto*, a complete handbook for Christian boys, to instil in them that spirit of piety which I perceived during my twelve months spent at the Oratory. He insisted that everyone should have a copy. I must recall an unusual method which he once used to make the *Giovane Provveduto* loved and esteemed. It was the end of the scholastic year, and he came to give us the Good Night in which he said that he wished to grant pardon to all and to set some consciences at peace. "It happens at times," he continued, "even here at the Oratory, that some boys come to complain about the disappearance of their *Giovane Provveduto* which others perhaps have taken (stolen, really) and you know that since this theft concerns something almost sacred, there could be a certain amount of seriousness, even though the thieves say they took it out of devotion, to be able to pray, sing hymns and so on. Actually, not only have I always taught you to respect the things of others, but I have also encouraged you to bring me each evening any lost property you have found during the day. This evening then, in agreement with those who have lost their prayer book or presuming their consent, I am going to give a plenary indulgence to all those who have taken possession of the said book, provided they make good use of it and promise not to commit this fault again. Furthermore, I recommend that our dear prefect and those in charge of the bookstore sell the *Giovane Provveduto* this month at half price for all the pupils of the Oratory so that they can all easily provide themselves with one in accordance with the title itself and the author's intention." The indulgence and reduction in price were welcomed by a burst of applause.

In these poor memoirs of mine I have made frequent reference to Don Bosco's spiritual direction of boys in general. But there is a great deal to be said regarding his method of encouraging and fostering vocations among those who showed themselves more docile, more generous in serving God and more capable of doing good to others.

I was to go to the missions in America and was preoccupied about the future of my brothers who were being educated in Alassio, especially the eldest, Ernesto. I talked it over with Don Bosco who arranged for my brother to come to the Oratory where Don Bosco could get to know him, study him and guide him. I then went on to ask him if he thought Ernesto had a vocation. "We have already had a chat," he said, "and we understand one another. I have taught him what to do in order to find his vocation and prepare to follow it. Let us wait a bit!" I was astonished and very pleased with the care our good Father took of the vocations of his pupils. "My brother is in good hands," I said to myself, "I can leave without any worries." Later on, Don Bosco himself gave me the consoling news that Ernesto had decided to become a Salesian and had received the clerical habit.

In this regard I shall recall another impression received from the words spoken by a glorious disciple of Don Bosco, Fr Cerruti, when he came to Lugo for my First Mass, bringing my three brothers with him from Alassio. I asked him if any of them showed signs of a vocation and he answered at once, "I do not know them well yet because they do not come to me spontaneously. I have had to call them in order to speak with them." From this I realised that there was a whole world of difference between the method of Don Bosco and that of the schools through which I had passed and where generally the rectors did not speak individually with the pupils. Don Bosco on the other hand not only encouraged the pupils to come spontaneously and confidently to him but also recommended his rectors to foster such confidence in their respective schools in imitation of his spiritual fatherhood.

Nor must it be forgotten that the year 1876–1877 was the first of the regular novitiate in the Congregation after the recent approval of the Rules. That was the time when Don Bosco had written his valuable Introduction with a view to making known, "the spirit that give life to the Rules," treating at length of vocation and of the means of following and protecting it according to the doctrine of St Alphonsus. Approximately a dozen priests came to the Oratory that year with a view of getting to know the Congregation and to enter it. Happy those who placed themselves entirely under Don Bosco's direction, who listened to him, visited him, consulted him! I realised more and more that the fatherly approach used by our Founder towards his pupils was used with even greater love and solicitude with his candidates and novices who already formed part of his Salesian Family.

Something else had already claimed my attention before I entered the Oratory: the life of the coadjutors. When I was in Alassio in 1875 I had noticed their prayerfulness in church especially in performing all their devout practices in common and in singing the Divine Office with the students. Fr Cerruti confirmed my admiration, saying, "These good coadjutors sometimes put us to shame by their virtuous lives so that we priests feel moved to cover our faces with our hands on seeing their edifying example." For me it was a revelation. The next year at the Oratory I was not long in discovering that this observance of the Rule, the prayerfulness and modesty of the coadjutors, their love for the house and for the Congregation came from a filial love for Don Bosco and from their fidelity in placing themselves under his spiritual direction. To please Don Bosco, to practise his advice to satisfy him by their good behaviour, formed the sum total of those good men's ambition. In fact, they wanted to be first in this love surpassing clerics and priests. I discovered in them a kind of jealousy in this noble competition. I remember how one day as some elderly priests surrounded Don Bosco with marks of filial affection, several coadjutors looked on this touching scene with a sense of slightly jealous children whispering in my ear, "Oh yes; but when Don Bosco was ill at Varazze it was we coadjutors who competed for the consolation of watching by his bedside the whole night!" I therefore considered the coadjutor as Don Bosco's confidant, almost the *factotum* of the house.

It must also be observed, however, that Don Bosco did not find his coadjutors ready-made but would prepare them long beforehand. We had a master cobbler at Buenos Aires, Bernard Musso who left Turin with me in 1877 and ran a workshop out there for 50 years. He religiously kept a note from Don Bosco, a fine example of ingenious ways the latter used to win the affection of his boys, especially if they gave hope of a vocation. Musso received this sign of fatherly benevolence in 1874 when he was just an artisan. It was sent to him from Rome where the Servant of God had very important business at hand. I shall quote from a copy which I made of the original:

My dearest Bernardo Musso,

I am at the moment greatly in need of the help of your prayers and those of your companions. Look among your friends for all those who wish to help me and lead them every day to Jesus in the Blessed Sacrament of the Altar to recommend my needs to Him. When I return to Turin, introduce me to those who have accompanied you on these visits and I shall give them all a beautiful souvenir:

Your affectionate friend,

John Bosco, priest

Digressing a moment, I should like to talk about the binomials which I heard Don Bosco use frequently. This is what I am calling the sets of two nouns which are used together to suggest two virtues which help each other. I will cite a few which impressed me at the time. *Piety and modesty*: Piety involved the word of God, prayer and the Sacraments; modesty, restraint of the passions and custody of the senses: piety, the support of modesty, and modesty the preparation and solid nourishment of piety. *Work and temperance*: work equalled love of duty and remedy against laziness, the father of all vices; temperance meant proper measure in food, drink, sleep and entertainment. *Reason and religion*: the former a human guide and judge, the latter supernatural to avoid overstepping the limits and forming a habit of looking for ease and satisfaction even though lawful. *Generosity and sacrifice*: particularly when it was a question of the glory of God and the good of souls. *Piety and charity*: these he suggested to all, including the boys, so that they might grow accustomed to doing good to their companions by example, advice, help, deference and patience. He wanted these virtues particularly in cooperators because, if in other times many confraternities had as their aim piety with fixed religious practices in view, piety had now to be coupled with the exercise of charity. *Prayer and work*: the old Benedictine motto *prayer and work* which Don Bosco made his own and recommended to his followers meant the blending of prayer and action so that the use of talents received from God might not be detrimental to the spiritual life or endanger one's eternal salvation. *Facere et docere*, to do and to teach: give value to teaching by example. *Cheerfulness and good works*: expressed in an algebraic formula [c + g - b (cheerful + good – bad)] = friend of Don Bosco. *Good confessions and Holy Communions*: to assure the life of grace and to progress in all the virtues. So too: *Jesus in the Blessed Sacrament and Mary Help of Christians*.

From my first weeks with Don Bosco, I was greatly amazed at the crowds of various people who were to be seen every day in his waiting room. To lighten his workload Fr Rua then began to receive some of the visitors. In addition to these personal meetings there was a great deal of correspondence. I was often with Don Bosco when he received the mail. He asked me to open the envelopes and hand him the contents which he read and annotated at once. One day, as he walked and chatted with me after lunch, he suddenly said to me, "Let's go to work!" He meant dealing with his correspondence. It was through personal meetings and correspondence that he spread his spirit, extended his work and increased the Kingdom of God.

Here I think it would be a good idea to describe one of Don Bosco's ordinary days which I had seen with my own eyes during the year I spent at his school. He rose before the boys and confrères in order to be ready in the sacristy to hear Confessions, and usually celebrated Mass at the altar of St Peter in the interval between the artisans' Mass and that of the students. At nine o'clock he went to his room where he drank a cup of coffee and looked through his correspondence. Meanwhile the waiting room was filling with people who had come even from distant places and who took turns entering his room. His experienced secretary, Fr Berto, had some trouble in rescuing the Servant of God when midday struck and they had to go to dinner with the community! Here Don Bosco was in the midst of his sons, with his beloved family. Although he entered the refectory very devoutly, holding his beretta close to his chest, he cast a gentle look here and there at the confrères, smiled and in special cases whispered a word or played a little trick like the time when he pulled my hair and said, "Nothing stands in the way." He liked to see regularity in community: prayers well said, reading well made and well listened to, and then spontaneity and friendly conversations.

Unlike the early days, Don Bosco in my time no longer went out after dinner to be with the boys nor did they enter the Salesians' refectory because very often there were distinguished people there talking to Don Bosco. As he drank a cup of coffee with some of his sons he would chat about useful, edifying and pleasant things concerning the Oratory, consulting them and giving tasks. That was the time when he won the confidence especially of newcomers; for us they were delightful moments containing a wealth of instructions and fatherly affection. Before going up to his room he sometimes took a short walk around the refectory itself or outside under the porticoes accompanied by someone who wanted to speak to him. Then he went back to attend to his correspondence or personal meetings.

The afternoon was also the time when he went to visit cooperators together with some member of the council or a secretary. Since he always had publications on hand, he usually brought manuscripts and rough sketches with him and he frequently stayed to work with people he trusted so that he would not be disturbed, a custom which Fr Rua also practised later. He would tell his companion to come back for him towards evening.

He also devoted part of the evening to his boys. He listened to them one by one, acquainted himself with their needs, gave advice and, above all, spoke to them about their future. On certain days of the week the boys of the senior classes went to Don Bosco to make their Confession more freely. During the scholastic year 1876–77 a young boy called Aime was in charge of regulating the entry of boys who wanted to talk to Don Bosco and of assisting them in the waiting room. There was no standing on ceremony; it was first come first served. On two occasions it happened to me that although I was a priest I had to wait until the boys there before me had their turn with Don Bosco. I admired this young boy's seriousness and goodness and the trust Don Bosco placed in him. He later became a true apostle in Spain and in Colombia where he died a holy death. Don Bosco had foretold that he would reach the age of 60 and this prophecy was fulfilled exactly.

Having started the day with his boys, he ended it with them. After supper and recreation, night prayers were said and then he frequently gave those classic Good Nights which produced the most salutary effects in everyone, all the more because they were always timely, insightful and connected with Oratory life. All retired to rest with those holy thoughts in mind, influenced by those inspiring words.

Don Bosco did not always rest at night. His publications and the needs of the work entrusted to him by Divine Providence occupied his attention during the night. At times in bed and at times at his desk, he dreamed about his Congregation, Oratory boys or other houses and often saw hidden things and future events in his dreams.

He sometimes said, "If Don Bosco were alive today or in such-and-such a place he would have acted differently, he would have adapted himself to circumstances, complied with government requirements or imitated such-and-such an institution." That is a mistake! Don Bosco would have improved his own institutions or schools in accordance with means and needs. He would never have sacrificed a single point in his plan of action. He would never have fallen short of his religious principles, of spiritual and corporal good works on behalf of poor and neglected young people. Never would he have changed his Oratory model in which one lives and acts in charity giving a Christian and secular education to working-class young people. Never would he have changed his method of recreation, of concerts, of helping his boys to love their school and their duties. Never would he have stopped being surrounded by the boys even during the holidays, which he tried to make as short as possible especially for those who offered the greatest hopes or who were exposed to greater dangers.

We hear people asking nowadays, "What would Don Bosco have thought of modern sport?" Modern sport with its multiple physical and even military exercises, with its competitions between one group and another, with its endless games before spectators, with the heated competition it arouses, compromising family life, detrimental to prayer and study, disturbing the smooth running of schools would never have tempted Don Bosco to forsake his own methods of daily recreations, weekly walks and occasional long outings. Don Bosco adapted prayer, study, useful work and moral and social education, any worthy institution or scholastic method, especially if imposed by the authorities or by national custom, and made them Salesian. He accepted anything and, in some way, made it his own.

There is another question we often ask, "Why did Don Bosco's words, smile, even a look have such an effect that they left indelible impressions on the mind, heart and imagination of those who met him?" We believe that there was something supernatural in this. Don Bosco had an extraordinary mission from heaven for the benefit of young people and the salvation of all. To help him achieve this God enkindled a burning charity in him so that his every act was like a light, which attracted people and drew them to God. In school life, in ordinary conversation, in spiritual direction, in advice given to those who visited him, in Good Nights, in his correspondence, Don Bosco was always consumed by the same zeal which inspired his fatherly affection, care and solicitude, his genuine goodness, his sincere desire to do good to others, and his wisdom and prudence which enabled him to win all hearts. This zeal, too, was the source of the vitality of his works, the source of that life-giving spirit which spread among the people especially the young and the working-class. The Holy Father Pius XI understood the great secret of Don Bosco from his very first meeting with him. We could even say that he, too, was fascinated by his personality. This is evident from the fact that by sharing his personal memories he has awakened in the whole Church the desire for an in-depth knowledge of the characteristic virtues and spirit which Don Bosco lived and left as a legacy to his spiritual family.

Chapter 30

The School of Don Bosco
Epilogue and Conclusion

The reader will have learned from these humble pages that the year 1876–1877 really marked great progress in the work of Don Bosco. For us it was a school of great learning, delightful supernatural discoveries that filled our minds, stirred our feelings and imagination. It won over our hearts and will, in short, filled us with so much happiness that we could almost say that even if we were without proof of the divinity of our holy religion, just seeing and hearing Don Bosco, spending a year with him would have been enough to make us firm in the faith and prepared no matter what the cost, what the suffering, to even go to the ends of the earth for the glory of God and the good of young people. Such were the impressions that we shared among ourselves after every conversation, brief lesson and every Good Night from Don Bosco. Hence it is no wonder that the whole of Marseilles, Paris and Barcelona were energised, running after Don Bosco to see him, to hear a word, to receive a blessing, to touch his garments and even to kiss his hand.

It was the year of model lessons, of non-stop performances, I would almost say, a continual time of learning at the school of Don Bosco. The Constitutions had just been approved. The regular novitiate was initiated with a large number entering it and a fine group of newly-professed with their special teacher, Fr Barberis. New works sprang up as though by magic: the Salesian cooperators and their Regulations were approved by the Holy See as a form of Salesian Third Order. The *Bollettino Salesiano* came into being as the official publication of the cooperators, putting them in contact with Don Bosco their Rector Major and universal Father. After the cooperators came the organisation of past pupils of Don Bosco to perpetuate the fruits of his school reproduced in all Salesian Houses and those of the Daughters of Mary Help of Christians. The Salesian missions were also begun in South America and ever more numerous groups of missionaries would celebrate the touching farewell ceremony every year at the altar of Mary Help of Christians. To further increase the number of missionaries, almost, is a result of that generous farewell, the Work of the Sons of Mary for late vocations was organised with the approval of the Holy See. Simultaneously, Don Bosco gave the final touch to his Regulations for Salesian Houses for the Salesians as for their pupils by inserting those valuable pages in which he sets forth and explains his Preventive System. During the same year he published his pre-existing Regulations for the Festive Oratories and for the other sectors added to this first institution. Finally, to crown all these events, the First General Chapter was held, consolidating by its deliberations the Pious Salesian Society and guaranteeing the success of the school of Don Bosco.

When there are not only lessons and eloquent speeches but when that mind and heart is the mainspring of great works, great institutions, great bands of working-class boys covering the face of the earth like the first blooms in spring, when oratories, homes and schools are seen with thousands and thousands of young people who eagerly reach out to this Father of the young and follow him, accompany him in all his enterprises, cheer him, carry him in triumph and proclaim him their true teacher, shepherd and saviour, then indeed one is tempted to repeat and apply to Don Bosco what we read about the precursor, "There was a man sent from God whose name was John. He came as a witness... that all might believe through him." Here is the relationship that connects all the saints to our Divine Redeemer. They were sent by God to the Church to give testimony to Our Lord Jesus Christ whose true and living images they are in holiness of life, in charity, gentleness, patience and humility.

More, perhaps, than any other visitor to the Oratory, the future Holy Father Pius XI with his fine mind understood the entire beauty, sublimity and generosity of the person of Don Bosco and so was enthused and edified by it that he publicly proclaimed his joy in having enjoyed his friendship in the early years of his priesthood. The familiar conversations he had with Don Bosco over a few days afforded him sublime lessons in holiness, activity and timely apostolic zeal for our own times, for young people and all others.

One may well consider me rash and almost vainglorious to have evoked these personal memories of a humble, newly ordained priest while many other older priests who lived for years by Don Bosco's side and shouldered the burden of work with him have left no account of their dealings with the Servant of

God. Such priests were very modest then, each one acts according to their own understanding. There are, however, two considerations: it is good to hide the secrets of the king, and it is honourable to magnify the work of God. I have manifested the little I saw and enjoyed of our common Father and Teacher to my confrères and codisciples and also to those whom God and Don Bosco himself entrusted to me as pupils and beloved friends. They are those dear family memories which Sacred scripture bids fathers and elders to pass on to their sons and grandsons and to generations to come. It is necessary to extend the school of Don Bosco more and more, that genuine family traditions be preserved, that the treasure we have inherited should not be lost but should enrich many other generations.

Now that I have come to the end, I feel rather dissatisfied in the knowledge that I have not succeeded in conveying the beauty, gentleness, attraction and efficacy of the School of Don Bosco which took possession of our whole being and won our hearts.

However, it is necessary to give the most realistic and exact possible synthesis of a very broad concept. It was during the years I referred to that the title *Opera di Don Bosco* [The Work of Don Bosco] began to be used, particularly outside Italy, for the Salesian Institute, that is, for the Festive Oratories, homes and schools and for the Society itself. Don Bosco did not want his sons to be called after him but after St Francis de Sales. This title, however, *Opera di Don Bosco* while respecting his wishes likewise satisfied those of his sons. It would seem, indeed, that the Servant of God did not dislike this title since he was truly the friend of workers and was himself a worker and co-worker for the good of society. The fact remains, however, that this name became popular and attractive, and carried on the early expression of Don Bosco's first young people who used to say, "I am going to Don Bosco, I belong to Don Bosco," to express the fact that they belonged to the family and house of Don Bosco. Even when the governments of the American Republics which were obliged by constitution to refuse admittance to new religious orders and congregations, upon hearing that Don Bosco was coming with a work and with workers, not only accepted him but favoured him and gave him generous donations. This is a genial and well-thought-out aspect of the school of Don Bosco.

But inside this body of work Don Bosco had placed a soul and spirit, infusing true life, i.e., the holy fear of God, as he himself says in the Regulations, by means of an enlightened piety and especially by means of the Sacraments of Confession and Communion. Don Bosco explained to an English government minister why his 500 boys studied in silence and another 300 conscientiously worked silently in their workshops without having to be rigorously supervised. "This," said Don Bosco, "is the result of living and practising the Catholic Religion."

When the Golden Jubilee of our Missions was being celebrated in Buenos Aires with a procession of 12,000 Salesian young people who walked smartly in their school and scout uniforms to the music of bands and the sound of trumpets while the whole population clapped and cheered Don Bosco and his work, a well-to-do lady was heard to say to the President of the Republic, "What beautiful, innocent, joyful and serene young people!" And leaning towards the other ladies added, "Don Bosco's young people are eucharistic! I am sure all of them received Holy Communion today at the beginning of this celebration." Since I was present beside them on the official platform I could respond:

"That's the way it is! This is a twofold eucharistic celebration also because it is a thanksgiving for 50 years of this life for so many young people, for so many families, fruit of that holy work."

I remember, too, how in the early days of the mission a certain senator who had been governor of the province of Tucuman came to visit our workshops with his son, an elegant young man. As he admired the shoemakers working earnestly at their benches, he, a liberal, said to his son, "Do you see? These boys are happy in their humble task. Do you know why?"

"Tell me why, father."

"Because they are working for Heaven. That is what Don Bosco has taught them." Then turning to me he added with real satisfaction, "Isn't it true that Don Bosco has promised bread, work and then Heaven to all his children?"

"Oh yes," I replied, "here we work precisely for this reward as Don Bosco taught us.'"

"This is just what we all need to do," concluded the senator, "namely, remember what is in store in the next world."

This episode reminds me of the great lesson given us repeatedly by Don Bosco in the Exercise for a Happy Death which constituted the basis for all the practices of piety in his Oratories and schools and among his Salesians, making it a day of special appeal and treats (extra at table, lotteries, walks). This exercise which included a general monthly Confession and Communion could be called a heavenly day, the day of the Kingdom of God in the hearts of all those boys. Such was the lasting affection and esteem of our past pupils for this practice that they established it in their centres as the characteristic of a good and faithful past pupil. The Exercise for a Happy Death produced an admirable effect in the region of Buenos Aires, called *Boca* [*boca* means 'mouth' in Spanish] which was once a hive of sectarians and even called boca of the devil. The good past pupils from this area assembled in August 1908 and agreed to pay tribute to their dear assistant, Fr Alfonso Glendi, by meeting every month to make the Exercise for a Happy Death. I had the immense satisfaction of distributing Holy Communion on the first Sunday of the month to more than a 100 of these past pupils, and even to 200 or 300 especially during the extraordinary visit of 1925.

It is time now to place all these characteristics of the School of Don Bosco under four distinctive headings which form the soul, spirit and life of his pupils and past pupils. Don Bosco formed in his young people a Christian way of thinking through catechism, Bible and Church history (theory and practice, examples). His Good Nights and dreams aimed particularly at teaching his listeners to think, judge and speak properly in accordance with reason and faith. Don Bosco always worked to form a Christian conscience in young people, in keeping with the holy law of God and of the Church. He obtained such delicacy of conscience from his pupils (through the ministry of sacramental confession) that fear of guilt and of offence against God replaced the fear of punishment. Here is an example: a boy approached me one day as I was leaving the study and said, "Father, such and such a companion accuses me of having spoken a bad word; but I assure you in conscience that I have never said such words." I called the companion at once and rebuked him because I was convinced that the fault could not have been committed. The boy smiled somewhat and then explained the reasons:

"You see, Father," he said, "that boy was seized with hiccups which were disturbing everyone, and he couldn't get rid of them. I had heard that a sudden fright is a good remedy for hiccups, and I thought about what would scare him most. As a result, I approached him and said, 'I am going to tell Father that you said a bad word!' The poor fellow turned pale, but his hiccups ceased at once! So you see my intentions were good." I brought the matter to an end saying: "Be careful next time not to frighten him so much because you could harm him!"

We may also assert that Don Bosco was very careful about the Christian character of his boys, that true character which is imprinted by the grace of God in the Sacraments of Baptism and Confirmation. He cultivated spiritual strength and fortitude by those special words, as they are called, because of the instantaneous effect which they produced on the will. Efficacy of word was the fruit and grace he had asked for in his first Mass. It was seen at its best when he was obliged to warn his sons about an individual or general danger which threatened. At such times, too, he received special enlightenment to read consciences and see the state of each person while Our Lady herself gave him clear personal mementos. The effect of the School of Don Bosco on the boys' characters was also apparent during the holidays and when it was time for them to bid a final goodbye to their educator. Those last mementos, those fatherly recommendations remained engraved upon the hearts of his boys, warned them of danger and made them devoted to the Church and to the fulfilment of their religious duties, distancing them from every danger.

The whole of this education was transformed into Christian life, that is, into the habits and spirit that make our whole being Christian in word and action, influencing everyone by our example, zeal and charity and by our concern for the eternal salvation of all people. Don Bosco promoted this practice of charity among all his pupils so that in school and at home, in clubs and associations they might be salt and light, as he said, by their advice and good example in everything especially in prayer and modesty. Here we see Don Bosco's pupil and past pupil prepared for that Catholic action which the Holy Father wishes to see extended all over the world organised by and in conjunction with ecclesiastical authorities for the spread of the Kingdom of Our Lord Jesus Christ.

This is shown at the beatification of Don Bosco by the way in which the past pupils promoted and organised general communions among three and four thousand followers in capital cities, thus presenting scenes of unparallel magnificence. Furthermore, additional proof was given by the behaviour of the past pupils, their constancy in work and in the exercise of their profession participating in all the works and associations of the Catholic Church. A well-known past pupil took a saying of Tertullian as the theme of an eloquent speech, "We are the children of yesterday who fill the world today."